SELF-ASSESSMENT PICTURE TESTS IN DENTISTRY

Endodontics

Edited by

Richard T Walker

RD, PhD, MSc, BDS, FDS RCPS

Senior Lecturer,
Leeds Dental Institute
Honorary Consultant,
United Leeds Teaching Hospital Trust

 **Mosby-Wolfe**

London Baltimore Bogotá Boston Buenos Aires Caracas Carlsbad, CA Chicago Madrid Mexico City Milan Naples, FL New York
Philadelphia St. Louis Sydney Tokyo Toronto Wiesbaden

For full details of all Times Mirror International Publishers Limited titles please
write to Times Mirror International Publishers Limited, Lynton House, 7-12
Tavistock House, London WC1H 9LB, England.

A CIP catalogue record for this book is available from the British Library.

Library of Congress Cataloging-in Publication Data has been applied for.

Preface

This book has been produced to provide a method of self-assessment for dental colleagues and students who wish to revise and update their knowledge and understanding of all areas of endodontic practice.

About two hundred questions and answers, many accompanied by illustrations, have been provided by experienced practitioners and teachers. Many of the answers provide information additional to that required by the question, and where appropriate, references are cited.

I would like to express my grateful thanks to the contributors for their efforts in furnishing the material for the publication.

Acknowledgements

The co-operation of Professor C E Renson, Editor of *Dental Update*, is acknowledged for granting permission to reproduce illustrations which have previously appeared in Endodontic therapy for primary teeth 1. Diagnosis and treatment, *Dental Update*, 1984; 11:154–166 by King N M, Brook A H and Page J.

Dr Alex Chan, Postgraduate Dental Officer in Conservative Dentistry, Prince Philip Dental Hospital, Hong Kong, is also thanked for his assistance in providing clinical material.

List of contributors

P V Abbott, BDSc MDS FRACDS. Senior lecturer in Endodontics and visiting Consultant, Faculty of Dentistry, The University of Western Australia. Practice limited to endodontics, The Perth Surgicentre, 38 Ranelagh Cres., South Perth, W.A. 6151.

G S P Cheung, BDS MDS MSc. Lecturer, Department of Conservative Dentistry, Faculty of Dentistry, University of Hong Kong.

B S Chong, BDS MSc DGDP LDS RCS. Research Fellow, Department of Conservative Dental Surgery, UMDS Guy's Hospital, London SE1 9RT. Practice limited to endodontics, 1 Lister House, 11–12 Wimpole St., London W1M 7AB.

A Dimmer, BDS FFD RCS FDS RCS. Formerly Senior Lecturer, Department of Conservative Dentistry, Faculty of Dentistry, University of Hong Kong.

K Gulabivala, BDS MSc FDS RCS. Lecturer, Department of Conservative Dentistry, Institute of Dental Surgery, 256 Gray's Inn Road, London WC1X 8LD.

A T Hyatt, PhD BSc FDS RCS. Practice limited to endodontics, 1 Lister House, 11–12 Wimpole St., London W1M 7AB.

N M King, PhD MSc BDS LDS RCS. Senior Lecturer, Department of Children's Dentistry and Orthodontics, Faculty of Dentistry, University of Hong Kong.

S A Manning, BDS MDSc FRACDS. Practice limited to endodontics, Milford Chambers, St. George's Hospital Drive, 249 Papanui Rd., Christchurch 1, New Zealand.

P R H Newsome, MBA BChD DRD FDS RCS. Senior Lecturer, Department of Conservative Dentistry, Faculty of Dentistry, University of Hong Kong.

C J R Stock, MSc BDS DGDP RCS. Senior Research Fellow, Institute of Dental Surgery, 256 Gray's Inn Rd., London W1X 8LD. Practice limited to endodontics, 1 Lister House, 11–12 Wimpole St., London W1M 7AB.

R T Walker, RD PhD MSc BDS FDS RCPS. Senior Lecturer and Honorary Consultant, Leeds Dental Institute, Clarendon Way, Leeds LS2 9LU. Practice limited to endodontics, 1 Lister House, 11–12 Wimpole St., London W1M 7AB.

J Webber, MSc BDS DGDP RCS. Practice limited to endodontics, 1 Lister House, 11–12 Wimpole St., London W1M 7AB.

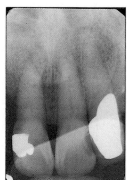

1A

1B

1 This middle-aged man was unhappy with his tender, discoloured, heavily restored upper right central incisor. The tooth had a history of trauma and internal calcification of the root canal space was evident (**1A**). Conventional root canal treatment was carried out (**1B**), even though there was no clear radiographic indication of the presence of a root canal.
Why was this treatment proposed for the tooth?

2 This fractured lower lateral incisor requires root canal treatment before placement of a post and core to support a crown.
What particular feature of canal morphology would you expect in this tooth after viewing the radiograph?
How common is this feature in lower incisors?

2

3 These cleared specimens of upper premolar teeth demonstrate the complexity of root canal anatomy. How is it possible that a standard regularly tapered canal shape, after preparation, is adequate to effect periapical healing when the root canal system can be so irregular and sometimes unpredictable in its anatomy?

3

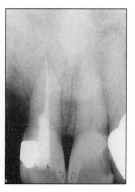

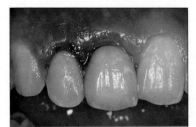

4C

4 This 19-year-old man was hit in the mouth with a hockey ball. The crown margin of the upper right central incisor was open on the buccal aspect but not on the lingual (**4A, 4B**). The tooth, which had an oblique root fracture, was extracted (**4C**).

Explain how the fracture arose. Would you expect to detect this type of fracture radiographically?

5

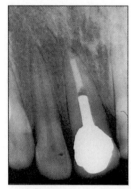

5 This man sustained impact trauma to his upper jaw. The upper right lateral incisor is mobile.

What type of injury did the lateral incisor suffer and how would you manage it?

6

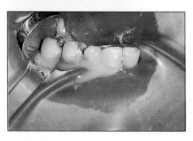

6 Drainage has been established through a coronal access cavity for this lower canine with an acute abscess. Under what conditions should this tooth be left open to continue draining?

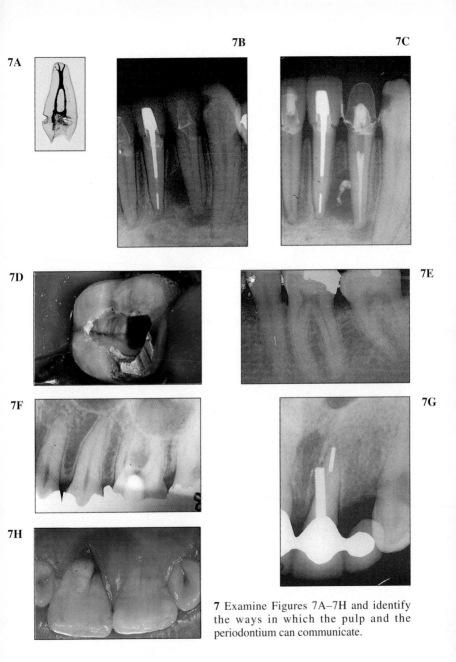

7A

7B

7C

7D

7E

7F

7G

7H

7 Examine Figures 7A–7H and identify the ways in which the pulp and the periodontium can communicate.

8 What are the resorptive conditions illustrated by the radiographs of the cases in Figures **8A–8H**.

9 In order to retain carious primary teeth, until they exfoliate naturally, as in this boy's mouth, it may be necessary to carry out pulp therapy and provide coronal restorations. Give five reasons why these carious primary teeth should be treated conservatively rather than by extraction.

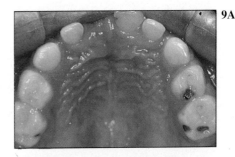

9A

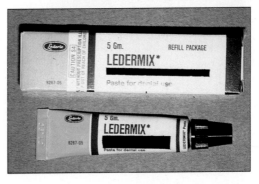

9B

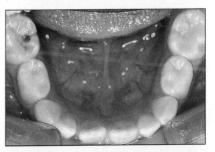

10

10 The figure shows a corticosteroid-antibiotic compound in a water soluble paste base. What are the two therapeutic components in this material and what are their concentrations in the paste?

11 A number of new root canal obturation techniques have been marketed which supposedly use alpha phase gutta percha. What is alpha phase gutta percha and what are its unique properties?

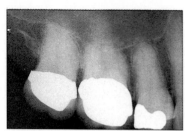 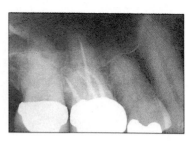

12 How many root canals does this endodontically treated upper first molar have?

Which root has two canals and what clue to the existence of two canals can be found on the preoperative radiograph (**12A**)?

Which roots of upper molars may have more than one root canal?

13 In order to avoid the type of vertical fracture illustrated, which of the following factors necessitate prompt, permanent coronal restoration of the crown of a molar following obturation of the root canals?

(a) Increased likelihood of caries recurrence around disintegrating temporary fillings.

(b) Vulnerability of coronal structures to fracture.

(c) Possible enhanced effect of coronal marginal leakage on teeth with poorly or partially obturated root canals.

(d) All of the above.

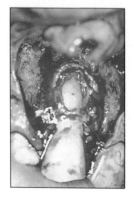

14 This lateral incisor with a non-vital pulp demonstrates bone loss around a lateral canal (**14**).

What effect does pulpal disease have upon the periodontal tissues?

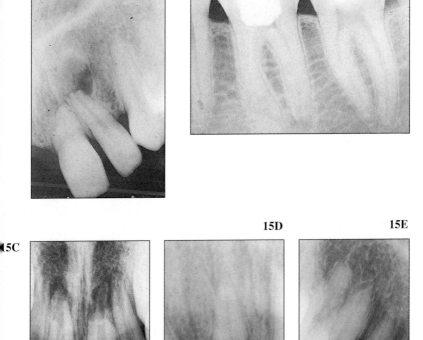

15 Figures **15A–15E** demonstrate the ways in which traumatic injuries to the teeth may result in subsequent resorption defects?
Can you identify them?

16 Under what circumstances would it be difficult to place a master gutta percha point to the fully prepared working length of a canal in which a matching file can reach the full length relatively easily?

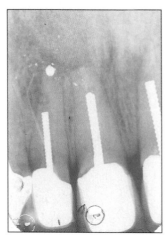 17A

17B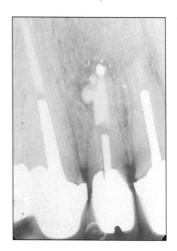

17 A periapical radiograph was taken for a patient who was complaining of sensitivity to chewing in the upper incisor region (**17A**). A discharging sinus was present in the labial vestibule between the upper right central and lateral incisors. Conventional root canal treatment was performed for the tooth (**17B**).
What was the likely cause of the patient's complaint?

 18

18 The Analytic Technology Pulp Tester has a number of features which set it apart from many other diagnostic instruments.
What are these features?

19 If it is considered that a pulpectomy cannot be successfully completed on a chronically infected primary molar in a 6-year-old child, then which of the following should be performed?
(a) Accept the situation and leave the tooth as a natural space-maintainer.
(b) Leave the tooth untreated unless the child complains of pain.
(c) Administer a course of antibiotics and then observe the tooth.
(d) Extract the tooth.
(e) Carry out a pulpotomy on the tooth.

20 A patient reports with pain and palatal swelling in relation to a vital upper lateral incisor. Radiographically, there is evidence of bone loss, and the presence of a developmental groove extending the length of the root is noted. Provided the emergency phase of treatment can be successfully dealt with, what is the long term prognosis for the tooth?

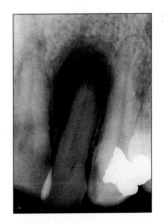

21 What is the function of this cast post?
(a) To strengthen and reinforce a tooth weakened through loss of vitality.
(b) To secure the core to the root, allowing placement of an extra-coronal restoration.
(c) To dissipate occlusal forces and thereby prevent periodontal disease.
(d) To seal the root canal from the oral environment.

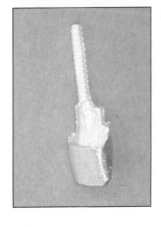

22 Amalgam is a commonly used root end filling material in surgical endodontics.
(a) What are the disadvantages of amalgam as a root end filling material?
(b) Are the following statements true or false?
  (i) Leakage studies have shown that amalgam root end fillings provide an effective seal against dye penetration.
  (ii) Leakage studies have shown that the use of varnish with amalgam root end fillings reduces dye penetration.
  (iii) Zinc free alloys are preferable for root end fillings where moisture contamination cannot be controlled.

23

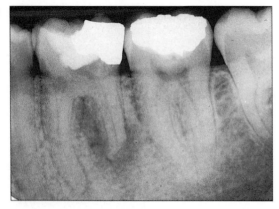

23 A radiograph was taken during routine dental examination.
What caused the shortened distal root of the lower left first molar?

24A

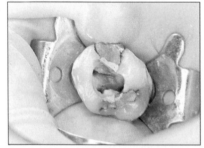

24B

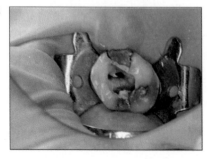

24 This upper first molar was opened and the three main canals prepared (**24A**). A second mesio-buccal canal was later located (**24B**).
What indication was there for the existence of this second mesio-buccal canal?
How would you search for this canal?

25 What has occurred to this mandibular first molar?

What may have been the primary aetiological factors?

How should such cases be managed?

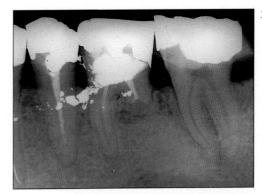

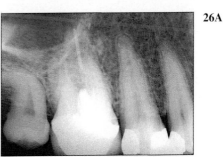

26 This upper right first molar appeared to be inadequately root treated (**26A**). It was decided that the tooth should be conventionally retreated (**26B**).

What factors did the operator consider before embarking upon retreatment of this tooth?

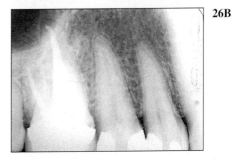

27 What are the possible causes of inability to pass a file to the full working length of a root canal, following some initial instrumentation?

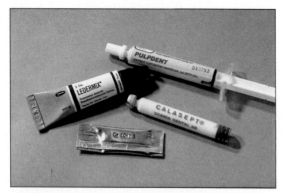

28A

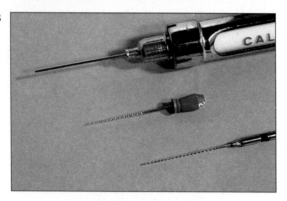

28B

28 Paste-type intracanal medicaments, such as those shown in **28A**, may be inserted into a prepared root canal using the items shown in **28B**.
What are these methods of application? Comment on their use.

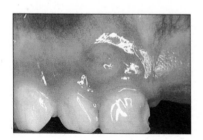

29

29 The presence of a buccal abscess suggests that this primary tooth is pulpally involved. Give four other signs of pulpal involvement?

30 What is this lesion?
What may cause a lesion of this type?
How should it be investigated?
How should it be treated?
What are the technical problems associated with treating such a lesion?

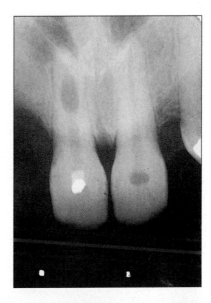

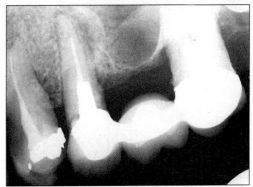

31 A patient complains of a spontaneous dull pain in the upper left premolar region. The bridge was sectioned and the upper left second premolar was extracted by the general practitioner but that did not resolve the pain.
What is the cause of the patient's complaint ?

32 What do you understand by the terms kilovoltage (kV) and milliamperage (mA) when applied to dental X-ray machines?
How do these factors affect the quality of the endodontic radiograph?

33

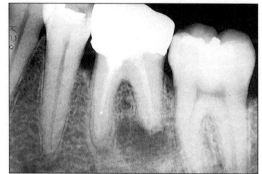

33 What caused the shortened distal root of this lower left first molar?
What treatment would you suggest?

34A

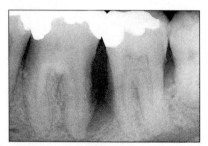

34 The illustrations show bone loss related to molars. In **34A** the lesion is of periodontal origin. **34B** shows combined perio-endo lesions.
How would you classify perio-endo lesions?

34B

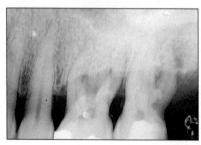

35 What do you understand by the term ALARA?
How do the principles of ALARA apply to endodontic radiography?

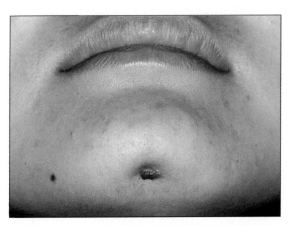

36A

36 This facial fistula of dental origin was excised twice (**36A**). The fistula failed to disappear until root canal treatment was performed for a mandibular incisor (**36B**).
How has the lesion come about?
What further investigations and treatment were carried out in order to effect a resolution of the fistula?

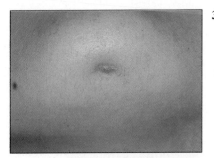

36B

37 When performing a formocresol pulpotomy, the cotton pellet placed in the pulp chamber of a primary tooth should be:
(i) Saturated with formocresol.
(ii) Left in place for five minutes.
(iii) Dampened with formocresol.
(iv) Sealed in place for five days.
Which is the correct answer?

    (a) (i) and (ii).
    (b) (i) and (iv).
    (c) (ii) and (iii).
    (d) (ii) and (iv).
    (e) none of the above.

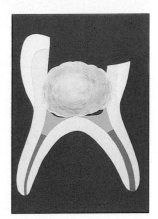

37

38

38 This is a lower second molar. What is the canal shape known as?
Is this feature more common in any particular groups of people?
How would you prepare and fill this tooth?

39

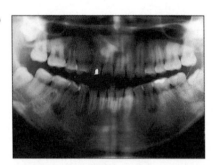

39 This panoral radiograph of a young Chinese patient reveals the presence of four premolars with immature roots and periapical lesions. What is the most likely explanation for this finding in a healthy, caries free mouth?

40

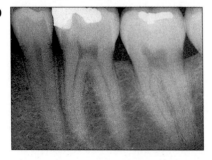

40 There is a 'white' line visible around the entire circumference of the roots of the teeth in the periapical radiograph of the lower molar region.
What is this and what is the significance of it in endodontic diagnosis?

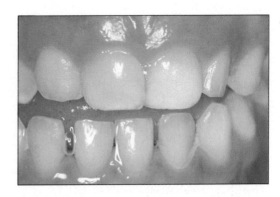

41 This 5-year-old girl has yellowish-coloured maxillary central incisor teeth.

(i) The affected teeth are non-vital.

(ii) She has the early symptoms of dentinogenesis imperfecta.

(iii) The pulp tissue of the affected teeth has been replaced by a dentine-like material.

(iv) The affected teeth must be extracted.

(v) Endodontic therapy is essential for the affected teeth.

Which is the correct answer?

    (a) (i)

    (b) (ii)

    (c) (iii)

    (d) (iv)

    (e) (v)

    (f) (i) and (v)

    (g) (i) and (iv)

    (h) (iii) and (v)

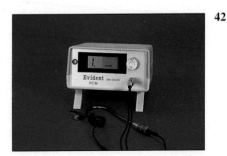

42 What instrument is this?
What does this instrument measure?
How accurate are these instruments?

43

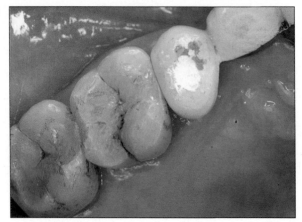

43 Root treatment has been initiated in the upper right second premolar of a middle-aged female patient who was complaining of discomfort in the upper right quadrant. The root canals were instrumented and dressed with calcium hydroxide. The tooth was temporarily restored with a reinforced zinc oxide eugenol cement.

When the patient was seen two weeks later, she continued to complain of discomfort, which was difficult to locate. She was conscious of pain on chewing and there was some sensitivity to cold. The teeth in this quadrant were not tender to percussion. The occlusal contacts were checked and the patient was reassured. Which diagnosis would you consider?
(a) Apical periodontitis of the second premolar.
(b) Traumatic occlusion.
(c) An undiagnosed fracture of the first molar.
(d) Atypical facial pain.

44

44 Gutta-percha points are usually coated with a root canal sealer during the obturation of root canals. What are the functions of the root canal sealer?

45 The lower right central and lateral incisors were traumatised four years ago. There is now a labial draining sinus which tracks into a radiolucency associated with these roots. What intracanal medicament might you use initially in this case and why?

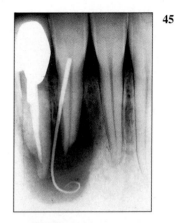

46 What subsequent intracanal medicament would you use in the case discussed in **45**, prior to completing the endodontic treatment, and why?

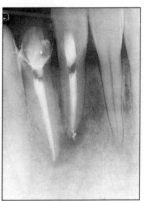

47 This lower right second premolar has been restored with a post retained crown. The length of the post might be considered to be satisfactory. What is held to be the minimum length of a post for a single-rooted tooth?
(a) Length of the clinical crown.
(b) Half of the root length.
(c) Two thirds of the root length.
(d) Three quarters of the root length.

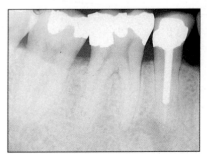

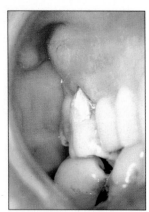

48A

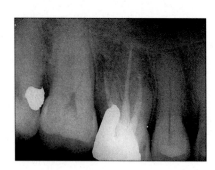

48B

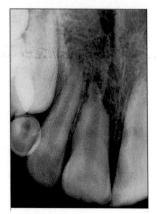

48C

48 A middle-aged man complained of pain and swelling in the upper right quadrant (**48A**). The upper right first molar failed to respond to pulp testing, and the swelling disappeared following root canal treatment (**48B, 48C**).
What is the likely cause of this swelling?

49

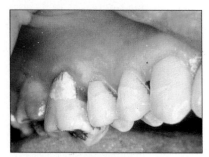

49 This central incisor was avulsed and replanted.
What is the nature of the resorption process?
What factors influence a decision to attempt replantation?
How should such cases be managed following replantation?
What are the indications for endodontic treatment?

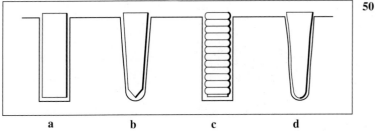

a   b   c   d

50 Which of the post designs offers the greatest retention?
(a) Smooth, parallel post.
(b) Smooth, tapered post.
(c) Serrated, parallel post.
(d) Cast post.

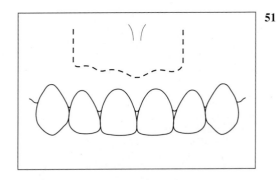

51 (a) What is this flap design called?
(b) What are the primary advantages of this flap design?
(c) What are the primary disadvantages of this flap design?

52 Some volatile antiseptic solutions have been used as intracanal medicaments (e.g. paraformaldehyde, parachlorophenol, camphorated chlorophenol, etc.) by placing a small amount of the liquid on a cotton pellet in the pulp chamber. List three reasons why this type of medication is not recommended.

53

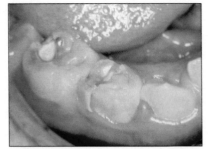

53 The pink colouration of this mandibular first primary molar is due to which one of the following?
(a) Haemolytic anaemia.
(b) Ankylosis of the root.
(c) Dentinogenesis imperfecta.
(d) Internal resorption.
(e) Congenital erythropoietic porphyria.

54A

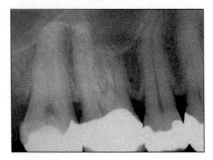

54 The periapical radiograph is the most useful diagnostic tool in endodontic radiography. There are two recognised techniques used to obtain the periapical radiograph.
Discuss briefly the relative advantages and/or disadvantages of the techniques used to obtain the radiographs.

54B

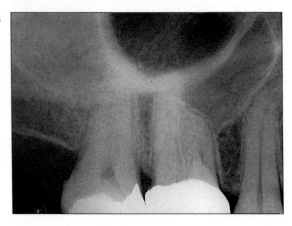

55 When would you prescribe an antibiotic during endodontic treatment?

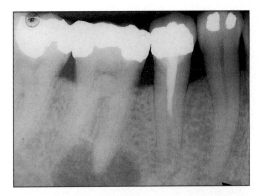

56 During the course of a routine dental examination of a 52-year-old woman, a radiolucent area was identified in relation to the mesial root of the lower right first molar (**56A**), which subsequently proved to be unresponsive to vitality testing. At the same time it was noticed that there were radiographic changes also occurring in the apical region of the lower right canine. This tooth responded to electric pulp testing and was not tender to palpation.

When radiographed two years later (**56B**) an enlarging radiolucency was identified. The tooth remained responsive to vitality testing and was symptomless.

What are your differential diagnoses and what treatment would you plan for this patient?

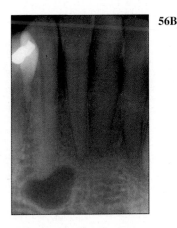

56B

57 The periapical radiograph demonstrates a mandibular first premolar with multiple roots and root canals.

What is the prevalence of mandibular first premolars with more than one root canal?

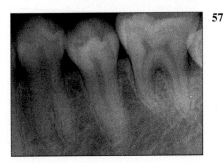

57

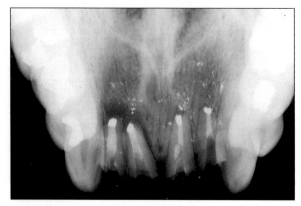

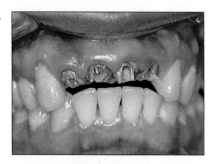

58 This young man had all his four upper incisors root filled some years ago. Periapical surgery has been performed twice to treat persistent sinuses. These have not been cured. The cast restorations in these teeth were loose and required removal and possible replacement. The patient has been referred to you for management of the failing endodontic treatment.

What treatment would you suggest?

59

59 Silver points, as obturating materials, have fallen into disrepute for a number of reasons, most notable of which is the tendency to corrode and produce toxic products.

What other reasons are there for not using silver points?

What alternatives have been suggested?

60 What anatomical structure is evident in the radiograph of this upper lateral incisor? Why has the previous treatment failed? What interceptive preventive measures can be taken?

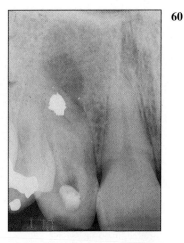

61A

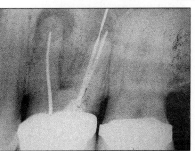

61B

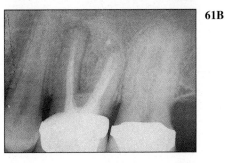

61 What is the nature of this resorption process involving the first molar (**61A**)?
Figure **61B** shows the tooth following re-treatment. How should treatment proceed?

62 Does the pulp tissue in the root canal system have to be completely necrotic for a periapical lesion to develop?

63

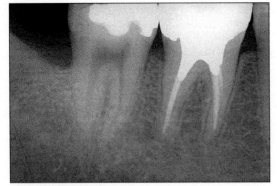

63 In recent years amalgam posts and cores have been recommended for use in root-treated posterior teeth. How do they compare to cast posts and cores in similar situations?
(a) Amalgam foundations are weaker and fracture more easily.
(b) Amalgam foundations are stronger and less likely to fracture.
(c) Little difference in compressive strength between both types, provided the tooth is restored using a crown incorporating a collar of metal located on sound tooth structure.
(d) Cast posts are stronger even when fitted with the type of crown described in (c).

64

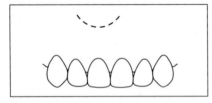

64 What are the disadvantages of this flap design?

65

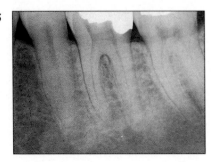

65 What are the radiographic signs observed in this picture which suggest the presence of a pulpal problem significant enough to warrant endodontic treatment of the lower molar?

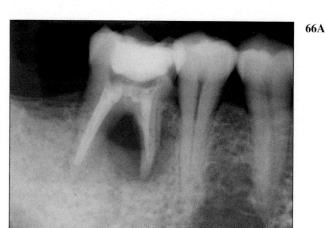

66A

66 A root filling was placed in the distal and mesio-lingual canals of this lower first molar (**66A**). The mesio-buccal canal was difficult to dry and remained moist. The obturation of this canal was deferred. Careful examination of the mesial root suggested the presence of a fracture (**66B**).

What are the possible causes of the presence of a persistent exudate in an instrumented canal?

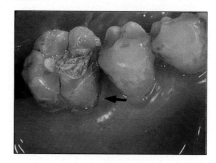

66B

67

67 What are the uses of this thermal device?

68

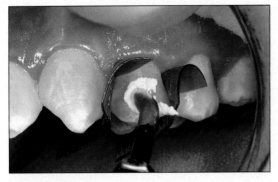

68 What is this clinical procedure?
What are the limitations of this procedure?

69A

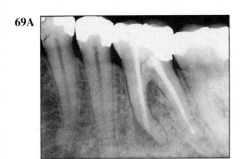

69B

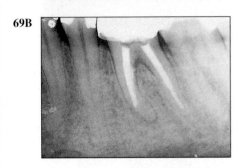

69 This lower left first molar was endodontically treated ten years ago but the mesial root canals were perforated in the apical third region. The patient now has symptoms indicating an infected tooth root and there is a radiolucency present (**69A**). Figure **69B** shows a follow up radiograph of this tooth 2 years after retreatment was completed.
What intracanal medicament would you have used to treat this case?

70 What is radiovisiography?

71

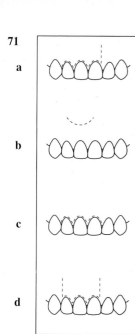

a

b

c

d

71 Which of these flap designs provides maximum access and visibility for endodontic surgery ?

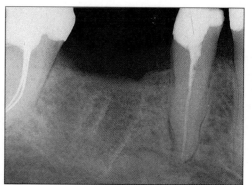

72A

72 Root canal treatment had recently been completed for this lower second premolar (**72A**). Pain continued in this area despite the treatment and the second premolar was sensitive to bite on.

A second canal was detected in this lower second premolar and following retreatment the pain subsided (**72B**).

What is the frequency of occurrence of second canals in lower second premolars?

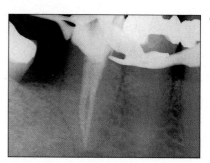

72B

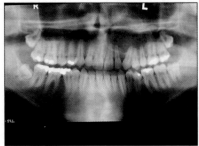

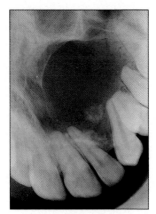

73 What type of pathology might you suspect in the panoral and occlusal films of a maxillary lesion (**73A, 73B**)? Post treatment radiographs are shown in **73C**.

What further investigations were needed to establish a diagnosis?

Why were so many of the teeth endodontically treated?

73C

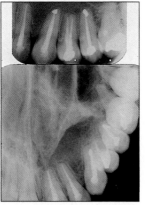

74 Which of these statements on post-surgical management is false?
(a) Antibiotics should routinely be prescribed as part of post-surgical management.
(b) The use of chlorhexidine gluconate mouthwash after surgery reduces plaque formation and aids healing.
(c) The possible postoperative complications in endodontic surgery include bleeding, bruising, pain and swelling.

75 What is the most important aspect of root canal therapy for achieving periapical healing?

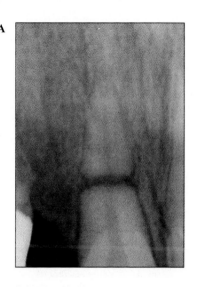
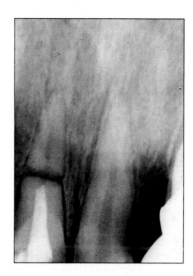

76 What has been the sequence of events in the treatment of this upper left central incisor?
What alternative management would have been preferable?

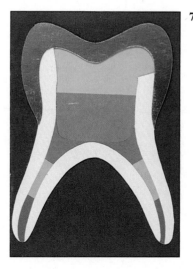

77 Following a formocresol pulpotomy on a primary tooth the tissue beneath the formalised zinc oxide, the dark brown region in the diagram, undergoes certain histological changes. Three different zones have been identified in the radicular tissue, each with its own characteristics. What is the histological status of each of the three zones?

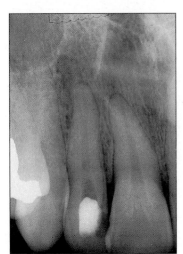

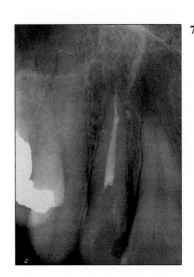

78 When viewing the pre-operative radiograph of this upper right lateral incisor (**78A**), would you have suspected the presence of lateral canals (**78B**)?
How common are these lateral canals and where are they likely to be located?
Are there any techniques available for their detection?
When root canal treatment is necessary how can they be sealed?

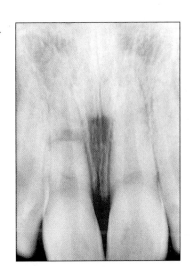 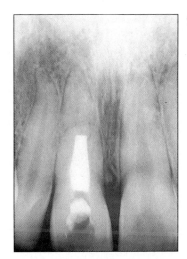

79 The upper right central incisor (**79A**) was injured in a sporting accident. The patient subsequently developed symptoms indicating a pulpless and infected root canal system in the coronal fragment of the tooth, which was endodontically treated (**79B**).

What specific endodontic treatment was performed and what intracanal medicament is recommended for this procedure?

80 Which of the following alloys, used as a post, has led to the corrosion evident in this extracted tooth?
(a) Gold alloy.
(b) Non-noble alloy.
(c) Palladium rich alloy.
(d) Silver palladium alloy.

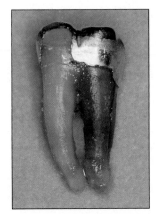

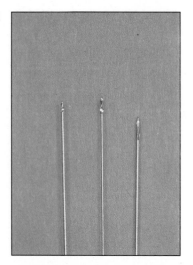

81 From left to right, identify the three instruments used in root canal preparation.
What design features do they have in common?
What are their uses?

82

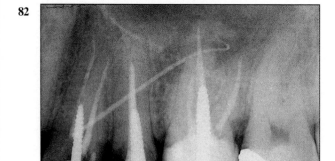

82 What is the diagnostic principle indicated in this radiograph of the upper left molar region?

83 The mother of a 10-year-old boy telephones the practice to say that her son has just had an accident and knocked out an upper front tooth.
What advice would you give to the mother on the telephone?
If the patient is brought to the practice what treatment would you carry out?

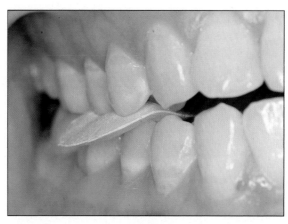

84 What is this test trying to detect?

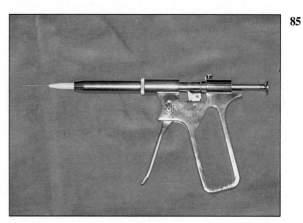

85 What is the purpose of this syringe?
How is it used?

86 A patient complains of a continuous pain on the right side of the face which becomes lancinating and severe with hot and cold drinks. The continuous dull ache is worse at night. No tooth is tender to bite on nor to touch. The patient has been aware of the pain for ten days and feels it is gradually becoming worse.
What is the likely cause of the pain and the possible treatment?

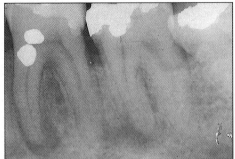

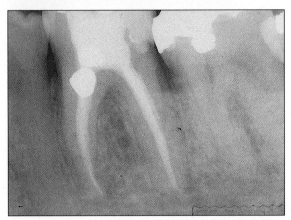

87 The periapical radiograph of the left molar region (**87A**) suggests that a lesion of endodontic origin exists in the apical region of the first and second molar teeth. The first molar was root treated and a follow-up radiograph of the region was taken six months later (**87B**).

What changes have taken place during this period and what is the diagnostic significance?

88 A tooth with a vital pulp requires a root to be resected to treat periodontal disease, would you:

(a) Resect the root and place an amalgam filling on the exposed pulp.

(b) Resect the root, leave the pulp stump exposed, and root fill the tooth 10–14 days later.

(c) Resect the root and leave the pulp stump exposed, the tooth not requiring root canal treatment.

(d) Carry out root canal treatment before resecting the root.

89 The formulation of Buckley's formocresol is given in the table. What are the therapeutic actions of the three constituents?

Formulation of Buckley's Formocresol	
	% by volume
Formaldehyde	19
Tricresol	35
Glycerine	16

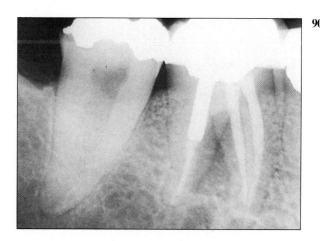

90 A patient complained of discomfort on chewing after root canal therapy and post crown restoration of his lower right first molar more than a year ago.
What condition is most consistent with the radiographic appearance and the patient's complaint?

91 There has been a trend towards the development of more flexible, safe-ended instruments for canal preparation.
What is the rationale behind this trend?

92A

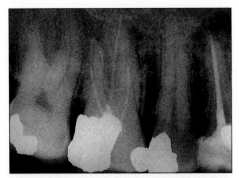

92B

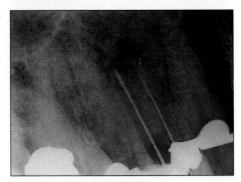

92 This radiograph (**92A**) suggests that the upper right premolar has been quite well root filled. However, there is a small radiolucent area periapically and the patient reports that the tooth is tender to bite on.

During the retreatment of this tooth a second canal was found (**92B**).

What was the likely cause of the continuing symptoms, and how can radiographic technique aid in early diagnosis?

93 A patient presents with a central incisor that has been satisfactorily root treated but the post has fractured at gingival level. What is the preferred treatment?

(a) Leave the post in place and use some additional retention, e.g. pins, slots etc. to allow a composite build up.

(b) Use a bur to drill out the post.

(c) Remove some tooth tissue around the post and grasp the post with pliers.

(d) Remove tooth tissue to allow the placement of an ultrasonic tip to facilitate post removal.

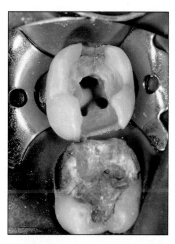

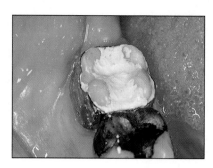

94 A lower right second molar was found to have a crack line running from its distal canal to the distal root surface following the removal of an MOD restoration and the preparation of an access cavity (**94A**). The buccal and lingual halves of the tooth could not be parted. A band was cemented to maintain the integrity of the crown (**94B**).

How would you manage the crack long term?

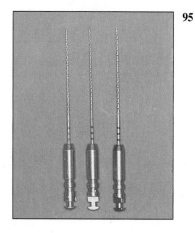

95 These rotary instruments are used in recognised root canal filling techniques. What is the principle behind their use? How may overfilling be avoided?

96 In an endodontic emergency context when and how would you carry out incision and drainage?

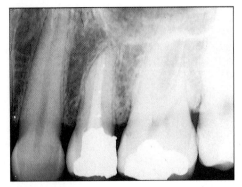

97 A 37-year-old lady has been referred to you following episodes of spontaneous pain in the upper left quadrant which started some years ago. Root canal treatment had been performed on the upper left second premolar but this had failed to relieve the discomfort. An apicectomy and periapical curettage had been carried out by the referring dentist. The pain recurred and hence the referral. Radiographic examination of the region was unremarkable.
What is the differential diagnosis of the condition and how would you manage the patient?

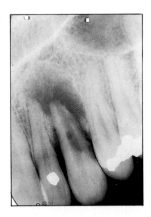

98 This periapical radiograph was taken one year after the maxillary canine was transplanted. The tooth shows marked inflammatory resorption, and the presence of chronic periapical infection with sinus formation.
What treatment might be prescribed to improve the prognosis of the tooth?

99 Radiographs are essential in three key areas of endodontics. Which areas are these? Briefly explain the importance of each.

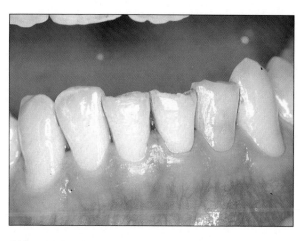

100 Which of the following is the most appropriate treatment for the root-filled lower left lateral incisor?
(a) Placement of a stainless steel post to reinforce the tooth followed by restoration of the access cavity.
(b) Non-vital bleaching followed by restoration of the access cavity with composite resin.
(c) Fabrication of a post/core and porcelain bonded crown.
(d) Restore access cavity with composite and place indirect labial veneer.

101

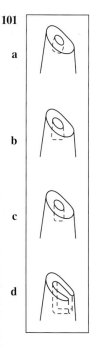

101 Which of these variations of root end cavity preparation have been used in surgical endodontics?

102A

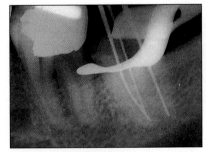

102B

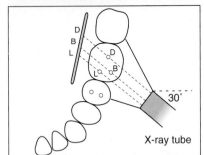

102 The radiograph of this lower molar (**102A**) has been taken using the 'buccal object rule'. The principles of this rule are illustrated (**102B**).
What is the importance of the 'buccal object rule' in endodontic treatment?

103A

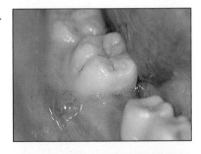

103B

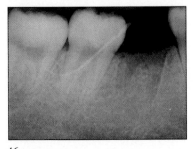

103 A 17-year-old Chinese girl complained of a recurrent swelling on the buccal aspect of her lower right second molar. The swelling was firm and there was a sinus opening near the mesial aspect of the second molar (**103A**). The molar was not tender to palpation or percussion tests and gave a normal response to electric pulp testing. A radiograph was taken with a gutta percha point inserted into the sinus tract (**103B**).
What was the cause of the patient's complaint?

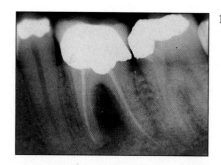

104A

104 The persistent inter-radicular area associated with this molar might have been of periodontal origin (**104A**).

What additional information would you require before making a diagnosis?

The lesion responded to endodontic retreatment (**104B**).

How many lower first molars have two distal canals?

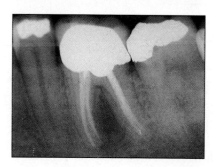

104B

105 A patient presents with pain and swelling due to a necrotic pulp in a molar tooth. Access is made into the pulp chamber and a discharge of pus is obtained. Would you:

(a) Clean the canals, place a canal dressing, seal the access cavity, and arrange to complete the treatment at a later date?

(b) Wait until the discharge has stopped, seal the access cavity and place the patient on an antibiotic?

(c) Clean the canals briefly, place a cotton wool pledget in the pulp chamber and leave the tooth open to continue draining. Arrange an appointment to continue treatment?

(d) Clean the canals and if the discharge is controlled carry out (a). If the discharge continues carry out (c) but arrange to see the patient in 24 hours when the canals are cleaned, a canal dressing placed and the access cavity sealed?

106A

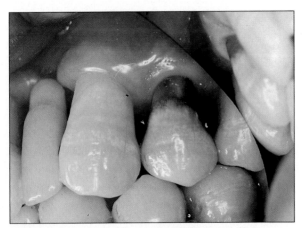

106B

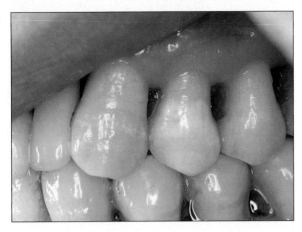

106 Bleaching discoloured non-vital teeth with hydrogen peroxide is an effective form of treatment which, nevertheless, carries some risks. How may these risks be reduced?
(a) Protection of fragile and delicate gingival tissues.
(b) Reduction of treatment time.
(c) Reducing the concentration of the bleaching agent.
(d) All of the above.

107 What do gutta percha points contain?

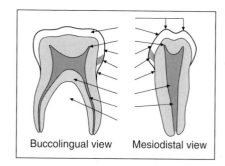

Buccolingual view   Mesiodistal view

108 The anatomy of a primary molar influences the techniques for performing pulp therapy and the final coronal restoration.
(a) What are the nine features indicated by the arrows in the diagram?
(b) Comment upon how these features may influence the endodontic techniques used in primary molars.

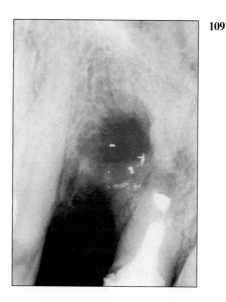

109 At routine examination, an isolated circular radiolucent lesion was detected in the alveolar bone in the region of the upper right lateral incisor. The upper right lateral incisor had been extracted more than a year ago.
What is the nature of the radiolucent area?

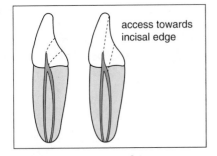

110 Why is it important to adjust the access cavity of a mandibular incisor towards the incisal edge of the tooth when the presence of two canals is suspected.

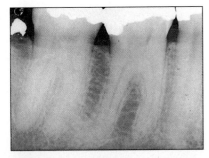

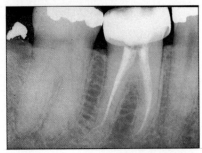

111 The lower right first molar has an acute irreversible pulpitis as a result of a cracked disto-lingual cusp (**111A**). What intracanal medication regime would you use during the endodontic treatment of this tooth?
111B shows the completed root canal filling.

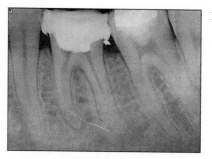

112A

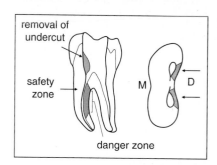

112B

removal of undercut

safety zone

M D

danger zone

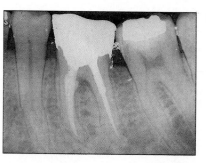

112C

112 There is a persistent tenderness associated with this lower first molar (**112A**), and bleeding in the mesial canals when the tooth is opened.
Perforation of the mesial root in the 'danger zone' is the cause of the tenderness and bleeding (**112B**).
How could the problem have been avoided?
The perforation was managed conservatively (**112C**).
What are the options if this treatment fails?

113

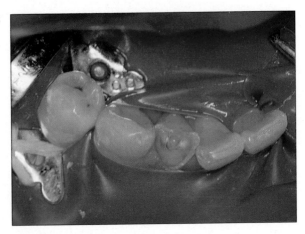

113 It may be difficult to place a rubber dam clamp on a tooth with a structurally deficient crown. The use of a split-dam technique is illustrated.
What other methods may be adopted to facilitate the isolation of such a tooth?

114

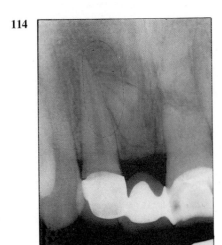

114 This radiograph was taken during a routine examination.
What treatment would you suggest ?

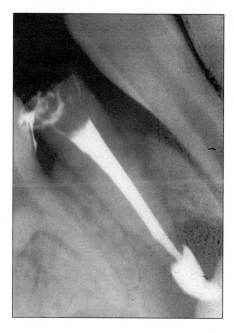

115 Whilst performing a pulpectomy some of the root canal dressing material (iodoform paste) was inadvertently forced through the apex of this primary canine. What action should be taken?

116 In the absence of specific contraindications which of the following local anaesthetic solutions would you choose for endodontic surgery, and why?
(a) Lignocaine hydrochloride 2% with 1:50,000 adrenaline.
(b) Lignocaine hydrochloride 2% with 1:80,000 adrenaline.
(c) Lignocaine hydrochloride 2% with 1:100,000 adrenaline.
(d) Prilocaine hydrochloride 3% (Citanest) with Felypressin (Octapressin) 0.03 iu/ml.

117 What precautions can be taken to prevent an alteration in the shape of the curved root canal during preparation which would lead to weakening of the root or its perforation?

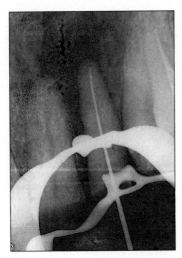

118 This working length radiograph (**118A**) apparently indicates that the tip of the root canal file is approximately 1mm from the end of the root.

Where is the correct apical position within the root canal to complete the canal preparation and obturation?

Using the diagram (**118B**) explain your rationale for the apical limit of treatment and indicate the various anatomic landmarks important to the correct determination of canal working length.

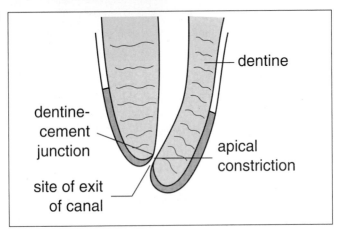

119 Following conventional root canal therapy, the periapical radiolucent area associated with a tooth fails to resolve. What are the possible explanations?

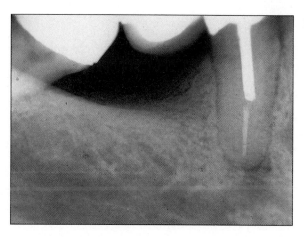

120 This radiograph of an apparently well filled lower premolar suggests that a lesion of endodontic origin may be present apically and that the case is failing. There are no subjective or objective symptoms.
What is the likely cause of the radiographic appearance?

121 An emergency patient has a swelling on the right side of the face over the mandible. The mandibular right first molar is tender to touch. The severe pain experienced for the past ten days has subsided over the last 24 hours. The patient feels better and there is no pyrexia. The patient is keen to save the tooth.
What is the likely cause of the pain and the possible treatment?

122

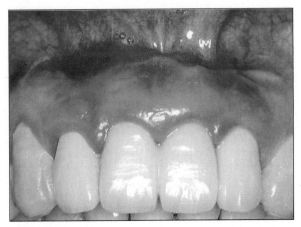

122 What is the cause of the gingival discolouration in the region of the upper right lateral incisor?

123

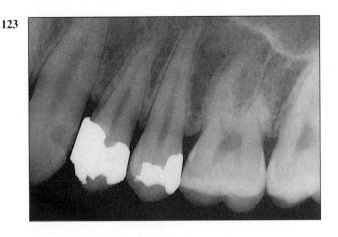

123 This radiograph of the upper first premolar suggests that the root canal has suddenly vanished at mid-root level, making instrumentation and obturation to the apical region difficult.
How would you interpret this apparent radiographic appearance?

124 Why are certain types of root canal instruments more susceptible to fracture than others?

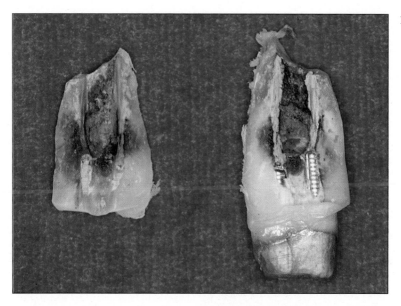

125 This fractured maxillary premolar was extracted because of the presence of a persistent sinus.

The tooth had been root treated three years previously and had remained symptomless until the tooth was restored with a post retained amalgam core and ceramo-metal crown.

An apical lesion developed six months after the crown was fitted. Apical surgery was performed without success and the fracture was discovered when the tooth was extracted.

What was the likely cause of the root fracture?

Where are the corrosion products derived from?

126 Which of the following indications for periradicular curettage are true?
(a) To manage continuing symptoms after satisfactory non-surgical root canal treatment.
(b) To remove overfilled and excess root filling materials.
(c) To remove infected periradicular tissue, facilitating rapid healing and repair of the periradicular tissues.
(d) To improve the apical seal.
(e) For excision biopsy to obtain a pathological specimen.

127A

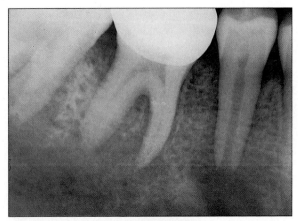

127B

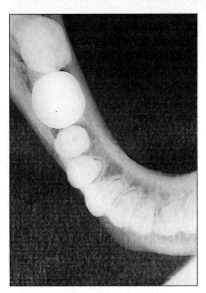

127 A 14-year-old girl presented with swelling in the buccal vestibule of the lower right quadrant. The teeth in this quadrant were asymptomatic. A periapical radiograph (**127A**) revealed an irregular radiolucent area associated with the lower right premolar and molar teeth. The apex of the second premolar was not fully formed. Bony expansion of the cortical plate was evident on the true occlusal view (**127B**).

What conditions might the radiographic appearance of the lesion suggest?

128 What are the principles of flap design in surgical endodontics?

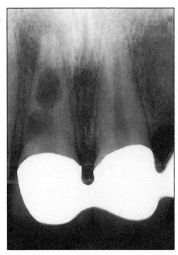

129A

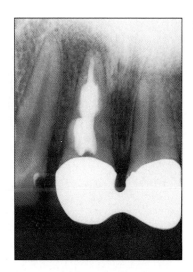

129B

129 The upper right central incisor has had internal inflammatory root resorption (**129A**).
What intracanal medication regime would you use to treat this condition?
129B shows the final root canal filling.

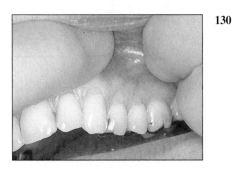

130

130 What functions does the diagnostic skill of intra-oral palpation serve?

131 A patient who has had the root canals of a molar tooth prepared two days previously presents in pain. The tooth aches and is tender to touch.
What are the possible causes of the pain?

132

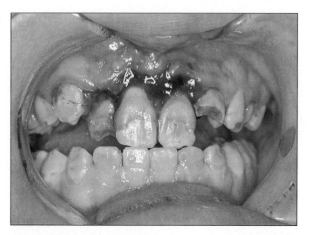

132 This patient reports with extrusive displacement of three mature maxillary incisors. The fourth incisor has sustained a coronal fracture not involving the pulp.
What primary care is required?
What are the problems of delayed treatment?

133

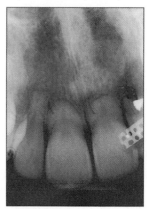

133 A 27-year-old lady was referred for an opinion regarding the 'progressive' root resorption of her upper incisors.
What do you suspect as the likely cause of the resorption? What treatment would you prescribe?

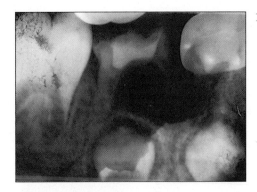

134A

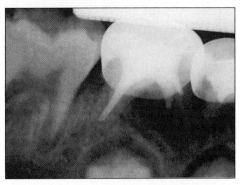

134B

134 The pulpotomy that was performed on this second primary molar (**134A**) exhibits evidence of failure. A pulpectomy was then performed to attempt to save the tooth. The second radiograph (**134B**) was taken five months later. Has the treatment been successful?
Give reasons for your answer.

135 Ultrasonically energised instruments have been recommended for a number of applications in endodontic practice. What are these applications and what are the merits of the use of ultrasound?

136 Which type of perio-endo lesion has the most unfavourable prognosis?

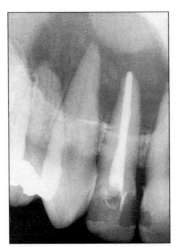

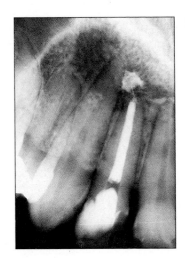

137 Large periapical radiolucencies can be treated by various means including conservative endodontics, surgical curettage or marsupialization. The upper right lateral incisor in **137A** has a large radiolucency associated with an infected root canal that has been previously root filled.

The case was retreated (**137B**).

What intracanal medicaments could be used to treat this case conservatively?

138

138 From left to right, name the three types of hand instrument.

Which hand instrument is least likely to be used for canal preparation and why?

139 In endodontic surgery, it is essential to use an anaesthetic agent with a suitable vasoconstrictor.

What are the purposes of adding a vasoconstrictor to local anaesthetic solutions?

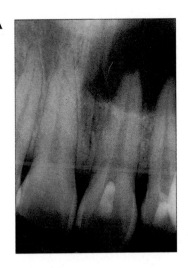

A

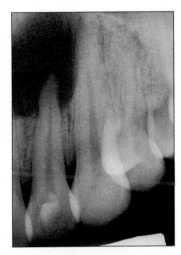

140B

140 A 20-year-old man presented with a large periapical rarefaction extending from the mesial of the upper right central incisor to the mesial of the upper left canine (**140A, 140B**). The upper left central and lateral incisors were non-vital.

Conventional root canal treatment was performed for the two non-vital teeth and healing was detected in a follow-up radiograph (**140C**).

How should large endodontic lesions be managed?

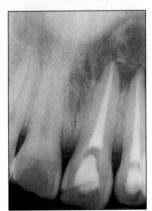

140C

141 Which of these statements about sutures are true?
(a) Sutures should be removed a minimum of two weeks after surgery.
(b) Silk sutures are non-absorbable and the fluid movements by capillary action cause the 'wicking' effect.
(c) A 4/0 size (US Pharmacopoeia) silk suture has a smaller size than a 3/0 size.
(d) Collagen is the basic component of plain gut (catgut) sutures.

142A

142B

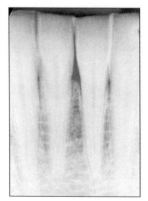

142 During preparation of the pulp chamber and amputation of the radicular pulp tissue in a primary tooth there is a danger of perforation of the floor of the pulp chamber (**142A, 142B**).

(a) What precautions can be taken to avoid this complication?

(b) What clinical signs may indicate that a perforation has occurred?

143

143 What is the cause of the internal calcification-like appearance in the middle third of the root canal of the lower left central incisor?

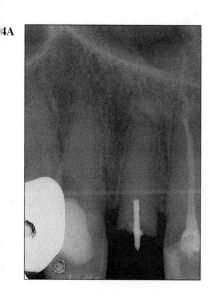
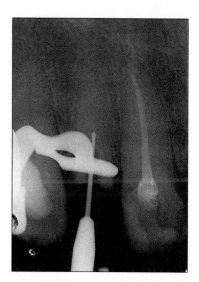

144 The radiograph of the upper right lateral incisor (**144A**) suggests that the root canal is sclerosed and there is no visible evidence of its presence.

In attempting to locate this canal using a bur (**144B**), discuss how radiographic technique would be helpful.

145 Which of these burs produces the smoothest surface obtainable following root end resection?

(a) Diamond bur.
(b) Straight fissure bur.
(c) Cross-cut fissure bur.
(d) Round bur.

146 Failure of root treatment can often be traced to inadequate access cavity design. What are the common faults?

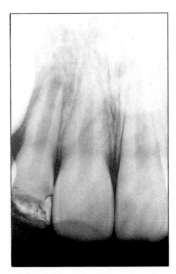

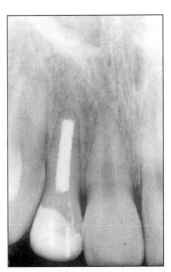

147

147 The upper right lateral incisor in **147A** had a complicated crown fracture when the patient was eight years old. A direct pulp cap was placed and the tooth was monitored until the patient developed symptoms indicating an infected root canal system.

What specific intra-canal medicament is recommended for use in such a tooth prior to the placement of the root canal filling (**147B**)?

148

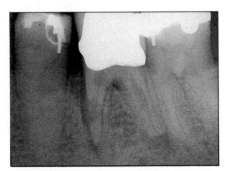

148 The radiograph of this lower left first molar demonstrates the presence of two differing types of resorption.

Describe the types of resorptive defect demonstrated.

Explain why the radiograph is useful in confirming this diagnosis.

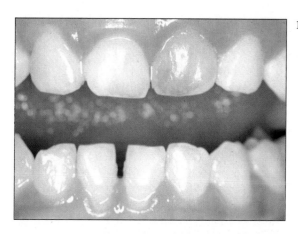

149 The maxillary left central incisor of this 5-year-old child is dark grey in colour. Which of the following is the discolouration probably due to?
(a) Hypervitaminosis during amelogenesis of this tooth.
(b) The administration of tetracycline to the mother during the second trimester of pregnancy.
(c) An as yet undiagnosed hereditary defect of odontogenesis.
(d) A traumatic injury to this tooth, which cannot be remembered.
(e) The recent taking of oral iron supplement

150 Which of these statements is true?
(a) A root end filling must always be placed after root end resection.
(b) The primary reason for bevelling the root surface following root end resection is to conserve root length.
(c) The long term success rate of surgical endodontic treatment has not been shown to be superior to non-surgical treatment.
(d) Teeth with fractured or broken instruments in the root canal should preferably be treated via a surgical approach.
(e) Teeth restored with post crowns are best treated by endodontic surgery.

151 What are the contra-indications to root amputation or root resection?

152

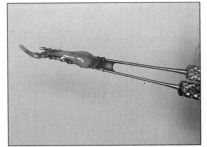

152 This large pulp has been extirpated using two barbed broaches.

What are barbed broaches made from and what are their other uses?

153A

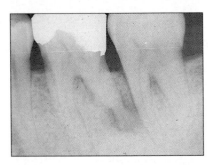

153B

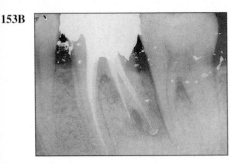

153 What features are displayed in the radiographs of this lower first molar (**153A, 153B**)?

How did these features affect the root canal treatment?

154 What guidelines exist for the size of apical enlargement of a canal?

What is the rationale for these guidelines?

155 Which of the following restorations should be placed in this primary molar tooth now that a pulpotomy has been performed?
(a) An amalgam restoration with pins for accessory retention at this appointment.
(b) An amalgam or glass cermet cement core and a stainless steel crown at this appointment.
(c) A stainless steel crown once radiographs indicate that there is no apical pathology or internal resorption.
(d) A glass cermet cement restoration at this appointment, followed by a stainless steel crown when radiographs show that there is no apical pathology or internal resorption.
(e) A stainless steel crown at this appointment.

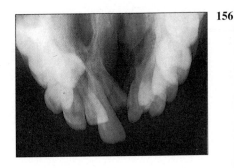

156 What is the large radiolucent lesion which has displaced the roots of the upper left central incisor and canine?

157 What are the disadvantages of the step-back method of canal preparation?

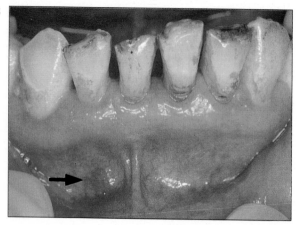

158 What is the small, round, bluish, symptomless swelling of the alveolar mucosa on the right side of the labial fraenum?

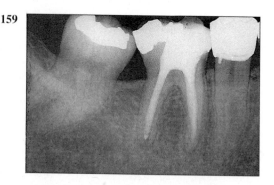

159 This root filled lower molar is painful on biting especially when the pressure after biting is relieved.
Is there any radiographic indication of the cause of this problem?

160 A number of different files claiming better flexibility have become available. How has this increased flexibility been achieved?

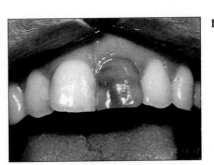

161A

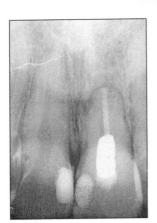

161B

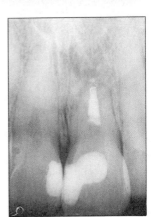

161C

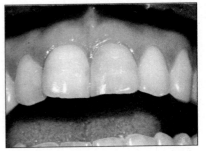

161D

161 A 25-year-old female patient presented with a discoloured upper left central incisor tooth that had been endodontically treated ten years ago (**161A, 161B**). The tooth was endodontically retreated (**161C**), prior to bleaching (**161D**). Why and how was this treatment provided for the patient?

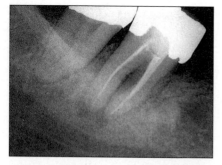

162A

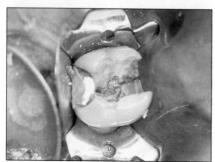

162B

162 This patient received root treatment for his lower right second molar (**162A**) many years ago and the tooth has remained symptomless. The construction of a cast restoration for this tooth has been recently recommended. On examination, oral hygiene was good, the tooth was slightly mobile and exhibited probing depths of 3mm on both proximal aspects. Removal of part of the coronal restoration revealed the presence of a fracture (**162B**).
Would you provide a cast restoration for this tooth? If not, why not?

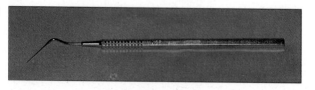

163

163 This handled spreader is designed to condense gutta percha laterally against the walls of the prepared canal. The diameter and general shape of the spreader conforms to the shape of non-standardised gutta percha points.
In order to achieve a good apical seal, how far should the tip of this instrument reach within the prepared root canal?

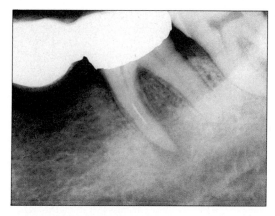

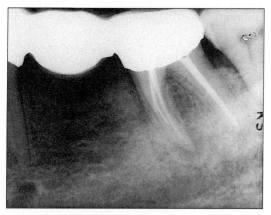

164 The lower left first molar tooth is an abutment for a bridge and a root canal file has broken and lodged inside the mesio-lingual canal (**164A**). The file could not be removed despite various attempts.

Can you suggest what the conservative treatment plan was for this tooth?

164B shows the completed treatment.

165 What success rates can be expected for:
(a) A pulpotomy using formocresol?
(b) A pulpectomy using iodoform paste as a final dressing, in a primary tooth?

166

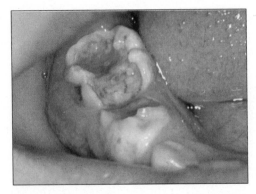

166 Give five possible reasons why it could be inadvisable to perform pulp therapy on a primary tooth such as the one shown.

167

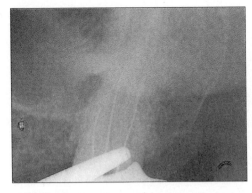

167 The working length radiograph of this upper left second molar provides little information regarding the apical extension of the root canal preparation.
Why is this the case and how can the problem be overcome?

168 It is sometimes found that, having prepared a canal to a size 15 or 20, it is difficult to place the next larger file to the same length. Why is this and what is the solution?

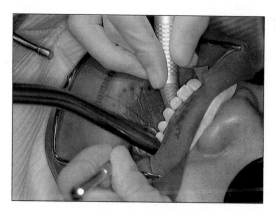

169 The use of rubber dam for the general treatment of patients in the supine operating position is not universally accepted.
Why is the use of rubber dam considered to be essential in endodontic therapy?

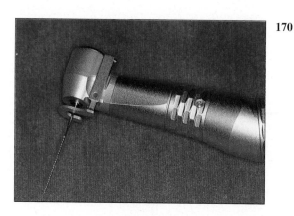

170 Identify this endodontic handpiece.
What action does the handpiece deliver to the file?

171 What are the clinical consequences of extruding root filling material into the inferior dental canal and what action should be taken?

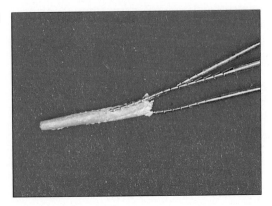

172 Single-cone gutta percha root fillings are generally easy to remove by screwing Hedstroem files alongside the point and pulling it out in an incisal or occlusal direction.

Removal becomes more difficult when a multi-point technique has been used. What other techniques of removal are recommended?

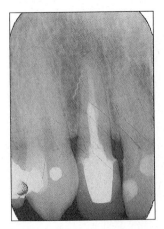

173 This gentleman presented with a buccal swelling adjacent to the upper right lateral incisor. The tooth had been treated and restored with a post crown. A radiograph revealed the presence of a separated instrument in the alveolar bone.
(a) What do you think happened?
(b) How would you deal with the problem?

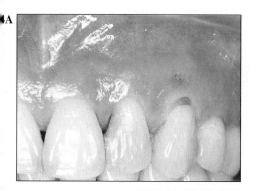

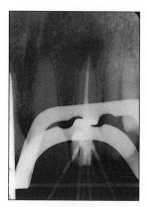

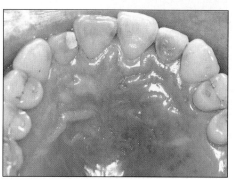

174 A middle-aged lady complained of an intense pain which started five days ago, following the root filling of an upper left lateral incisor. The tooth was slightly tender to percussion and palpation in the apical region. A sinus-like lesion was noted on the attached gingivae near the buccal aspect of the upper left canine (**174A**). The post-obturation radiograph showed an extrusion of root canal sealer beyond the apical foramen (**174B**). Palatal lesions similar to the buccal lesion were also observed (**174C**).
What is the likely cause of the patient's complaint?

175 After a paste medicament has been placed in a root canal, how would you expect it to work?

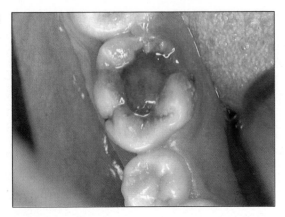

176 A young patient presents with a reddish overgrowth of tissue protruding from carious exposure in a lower molar. What is the nature of this lesion and most probable diagnosis?
If the tooth were to be conserved what treatment is indicated?

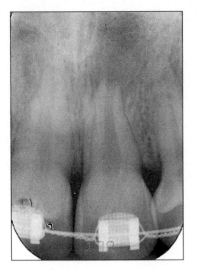

177 What difficulties might be encountered in treating this upper left central incisor.
What means are employed to overcome these difficulties?

178 Instrumentation of root canals results in the formation of a smear layer on the dentine wall.
What does this consist of and what is its significance?

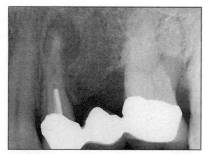

179A

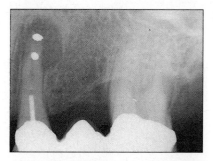

179B

179 This lady presented with a sinus tract buccal to the upper left first premolar tooth, which was part of a bridge (179A). Root end resection and root end filling were performed (179B). The sinus returned and surgery was deemed a failure evidenced by the gutta percha cone radiograph (179C).
(a) What are the treatment options for this tooth?
(b) What is the treatment of choice?

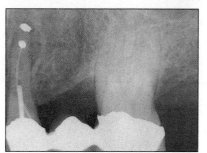

179C

180 Is it possible for a tooth with a completely necrotic pulp to have a radiographically intact periodontal ligament space?

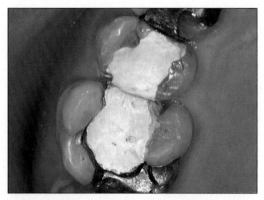

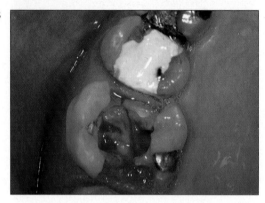

181 This patient returned after the first visit for root treatment of the upper right first molar. She complained of mild discomfort on chewing and a loose temporary restoration (**181A**).
Removal of the restoration revealed a fracture line running mesio-distally (**181B**). Why has the tooth fractured?
What are the treatment options?

182 Marsupialization (decompression) is used to treat large periradicular lesions.
(a) What are the advantages of marsupialization versus enucleation when treating large periradicular lesions?
(b) What are the possible disadvantages?

183 This periapical radiograph was taken during a periodic review examination. Two isolated, radiopaque masses can be seen at the root ends of the central and lateral incisors.

Can you identify the materials which have given rise to the radiopacities?

183

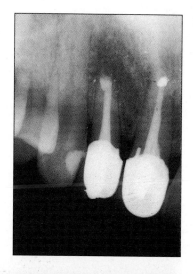

184

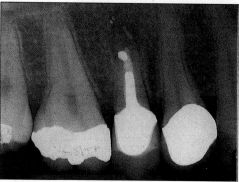

184 A young lady attended complaining of buccal tenderness and discomfort around the upper right second premolar region. Three years ago surgical endodontics was carried out on this tooth by another practitioner.
(a) Why has surgical treatment failed?
(b) What treatment options remain?
(c) Which treatment option would you choose and why?

185 Give a list of the tests and procedures that are available to locate the cause of dental pain?

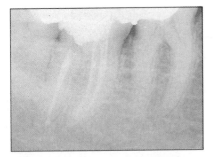

186A

186 This root filled lower molar (**186A**) remained symptom free until the patient returned three months after the placement of the final restoration, complaining of pain and a buccal swelling.

A radiograph (**186B**) reveals a radiolucency within the furcation. What is the likely diagnosis and cause of the patient's problem?

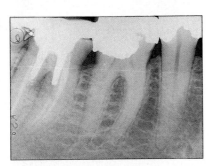

186B

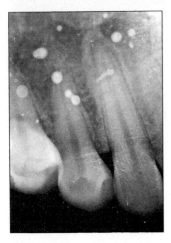

187

187 What are the small round opacities near the apices of the upper right canine and premolar on this periapical radiograph?

188 List four functions of intracanal medicaments.

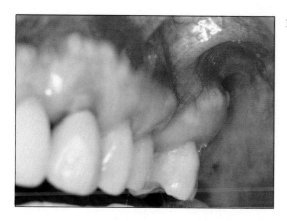

189 A patient presents with painless gingival swellings on the buccal aspect of the upper left quadrant. On palpation, the swellings were hard but there was no tenderness.

What would you consider to be the underlying cause?

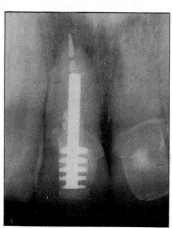

190 This patient was referred for treatment of a buccal swelling and discharging sinus tract related to the upper right central incisor.

(a) What can you see on the radiograph of the tooth?

(b) What treatment would you provide?

191 Which of the following is the most appropriate instrument for removing gutta percha from the root canal?

(a) Peeso-type reamer.

(b) Tapered fissure bur running at slow speed.

(c) Tapered fissure bur running at high speed.

(d) No. 4 round bur at slow speed.

192

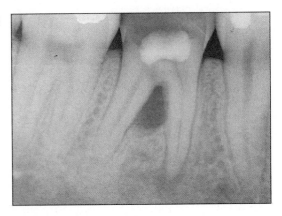

192 A perforation 1–2mm in diameter occurs in the floor of the pulp chamber of a molar tooth. What treatment would you consider and what is the prognosis when:
(a) The perforation is long standing and the radiograph shows a furcation involvement (as illustrated).
(b) The perforation has just occurred.

193

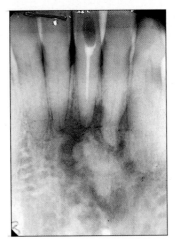

193 This periapical radiograph of the lower anterior teeth of a middle-aged woman of African origin appears to show a periapical radiolucency related to a previously root treated lower left central incisor. The pulps of the other incisors respond normally to pulp testing.
What is the differential diagnosis of this condition?

194 What factors dictate the desired shape of the prepared root canal?

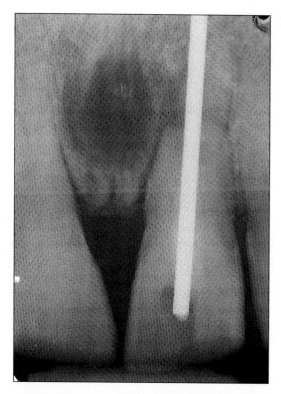

195 This gentleman attended complaining of a swelling between his upper central incisors. He had noticed that the swelling had increased in size over a period of time, but was not painful.
(a) What can you see from the radiograph?
(b) What treatment would you propose.

196 (a) What are the indications for surgical endodontics?
(b) What are the local contra-indications for surgical endodontics?
(c) What factors should be considered before deciding to carry out surgical endodontics?

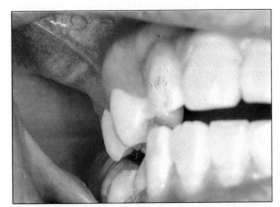

197A

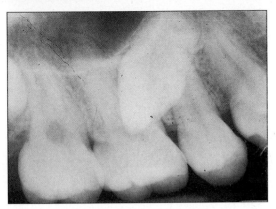

197B

197 A 16-year-old girl attended for a routine dental examination. On examination, a submucosal mass was detected in the buccal vestibule of the upper right quadrant (**197A**). The swelling was hard and the patient reported slight discomfort on firm digital pressure. There was no submandibular lymphadenopathy.

A periapical radiograph (**197B**) revealed the presence of an unerupted canine.

Would you expect signs of inflammation?

How should the position of this unerupted tooth be verified?

198 Which type of perio-endo lesion has the most favourable prognosis?

199 A patient complains of a sharp stabbing pain, on the right side of his mouth, which occurs sometimes on eating. No tooth is tender to percussion and there is nothing evident either clinically or on a periapical radiograph.
What tests or procedures would you carry out to investigate the cause of the pain?

200 How may the state of the pulp, in the situation of **199**, be diagnosed?

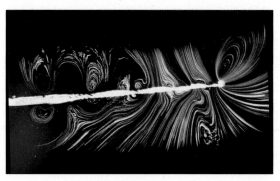

201

201 An instrument vibrating ultrasonically in an irrigant-flooded canal space produces severe turbulence of the irrigant.
What is this effect called?

ANSWERS

1 Even in the radiographic absence of a root canal, conventional (orthograde) root canal treatment is indicated.

Although the root canal appears radiographically to be calcified, it should not be assumed that the patency of the canal has been lost. It is possible to locate the canal and treat it endodontically (Schindler and Gullickson, 1988). Root canal treatment was carried out with the aid of fine hand instruments and an EDTA containing lubrication paste (**1B**).

2 This lower incisor has a bifurcated canal. The radiographic clues are:
The canal appears to go down one side of the root and suddenly narrows in the mid-root area.

The adjacent incisor has a clearly bifurcated canal.

Over 40% of lower incisors may have more than one canal (Benjamin and Dowson, 1974). The lingual canal is the canal most commonly missed.

3 This is probably because healing is dependent upon a relative reduction in bacterial contamination of the root canal system and a change in the pathogenicity of the bacterial flora, rather than the achievement of a sterile environment. In relatively simple tubular canals the prepared canal may completely encompass the unprepared canal and therefore effect debridement and decontamination mainly by the mechanical action of files. In root canal systems with more complicated shapes it is likely that the prepared shape only partly encompasses the canal system. In such cases success is dependent upon the mechanical preparation reducing the bacterial flora and rendering it less pathogenic. The use of an antibacterial irrigant, root canal medicament and root filling may be important in aiding this change.

4 The tooth was restored with a post retained ceramo-metal crown. The impact force on the post-crown caused the oblique fracture parting the remaining root into buccal and lingual fragments (**4C**). The orientation of the fracture line does not lend itself to ready detection by radiography.

5 This is an example of extrusive luxation. The extrusion should be reduced and the tooth splinted for two to three weeks. The tooth should be reviewed regularly. Over 50% of permanent teeth suffering extrusive luxation develop pulpal necrosis, necessitating root canal therapy at a later date.

6 The tooth may be left on open drainage if the discharge is uncontrollable. The patient should be reviewed within 24 hours, so that the canal can be thoroughly cleaned and sealed.

7 (a) Apical foramina and lateral canals. The apical portion of the root canal usually divides into an apical delta so that there are a number of apical foramina (**7A**). Lateral canals provide another connection between the pulpal and periodontal tissues. A large lateral lesion associated with a lateral incisor (**7B**) becomes apparent when the tooth is root treated (**7C**). Burch and Hulen (1974) reported that 76% of all molars presented openings into the furcation area.

(b) Dentinal tubules. Dentinal tubules may allow solutes to pass through in either direction and so are a source of communication between the pulp and the periodontal tissues (Walton and Torabinejad, 1989).

(c) Root fracture. Vertical root fractures inevitably become infected because of the passage of micro-organisms from the oral cavity or from the pulp. The fractures may be difficult to diagnose as they do not show on the radiograph in the early stages. This fracture on the mesial wall of the first molar (**7D**) is not apparent on the radiograph (**7E**).

(d) Iatrogenic perforation. Looking for a fine canal on the floor of a pulp chamber in a premolar or molar tooth using a bur (**7F**), or drilling a post hole (**7G**) are two common causes of iatrogenic perforation.

(e) Congenital groove. This is a developmental defect resulting from an infolding of the enamel organ during proliferation. These grooves are usually situated on the palatal aspect of maxillary lateral incisors or occasionally centrals (**7H**). The buccal surface is rarely affected. The depth of the groove varies extending from the cingulum and passing down the palatal aspect of the root for a few millimetres or almost to the apex. The groove may be deep enough to communicate with the root pulp.

8 The radiographs display different types of resorption.
    8A External inflammatory resorption – chronic apical periodontitis.
    8B External replacement resorption.
    8C External surface resorption.
    8D Internal inflammatory resorption.
    8E Internal replacement resorption.

8F Pressure resorption related to a tumour (Ameloblastoma).
8G Pressure resorption related to a previously impacted tooth.
8H Root end resorption related to excessive orthodontic force application.

The resorption of the dental calcified tissue is usually due to the activity of osteoclasts, which differentiate, and which are stimulated to activity by mediators of inflammation. The most common causes of inflammatory change arising at the junction between the dental calcified and vascular connective tissues are infection and trauma. Infection may be either acute or chronic and may affect either the dental pulp or the periodontal attachment apparatus. As the physiological resorption of significant volumes of calcified tissues requires several weeks or months in most cases, resorption of this type is usually associated with chronic infection with organisms of low grade virulence in asymptomatic conditions.

Acute trauma (i.e. single brief episodes) may result in small, reversible resorption lesions of cementum as a result of inflammation, but more commonly, trauma results in resorption due to a process of physiological remodelling of the calcified tissues. This disruption of the periodontium in subluxation and in replantation may lead to ankylosis and replacement resorption (i.e. the replacement of cementum and dentine with bone). Chronic excessive force (e.g. that arising during orthodontic tooth movement, or in trauma from occlusion, may also lead to the remodelling of the dental hard tissues but not to replacement resorption.

Chemical trauma (e.g. the use of powerful oxidising agents in the internal bleaching of non-vital teeth) may produce external, usually cervical, resorption patterns. Resorption may also occur as a result of intrinsically developed pressure generated by cysts, tumours or impacted teeth. Finally, resorption of tooth tissue, both internal and external also arises from unknown (idiopathic) causes.

9 (a) Maintenance of the arch length.
(b) Prevention of damage to the succeeding permanent teeth.
(c) To prevent the child from suffering unnecessary pain and infection.
(d) To maintain masticatory function.
(e) Avoidance of the psychological and physical trauma associated with the extraction of a tooth, especially in a young child.

10 The two therapeutic components and their concentrations are:
(a) Triamcinolone acetonide – 1.0% (a corticosteroid)
(b) Demethylchlortetracycline – 3.21% (also called demeclocycline, a tetracycline antibiotic).

11 Gutta percha is a polymer of isoprene as is natural rubber. Both materials are therefore isomers of poly isoprene, natural rubber is cis-polyisoprene and gutta percha is trans-polyisoprene. Trans-polyisoprene has two crystalline stereo forms termed alpha and beta phase. Alpha phase has a more linear molecular structure than beta phase.

Most of the commercially available gutta percha points contain the beta form. Some of the new thermoplastic techniques reputedly contain the alpha form. It has been claimed that this form when plasticised has a tacky nature and better flow characteristics. Although it has been shown that these molecular phases persist within at least certain temperature limits in the plasticised form, there is no published evidence that they possess the claimed physical properties. Nevertheless, the marketed products do seem to have good flow characteristics and whether this is due to other factors is not clear.

12 There are four root canals in this upper molar, with two root canals in the mesio-buccal root (**12B**). The mesio-buccal root on the radiograph (**12A**) appears wider than the disto-buccal and is likely to have more than one canal.

The mesio-buccal root of upper first molars can have more than one canal in over 55% of cases (Vertucci, 1974). The palatal root will have two canals or a figure-8-shaped canal only occasionally. The disto-buccal root will rarely have more than one canal.

13 (d). In an excellent paper on the subject, Safavi *et al.* (1987) found that successful endodontic treatment was more likely in teeth with permanent restorations compared with those with temporary restorations. It would appear sensible to provide a permanent restoration sooner rather than later.

14 Pulpal disease can spread from the pulp via one or more of the communication channels to involve the attachment apparatus. The disease results in the replacement of the periodontal ligament with inflammatory tissue usually with accompanying resorption of the alveolar bone.

15 (a) Acute force.
(i) Pulpal necrosis and infection.

Any force sufficient to disrupt the integrity of the apical blood vessels may lead to pulpal necrosis. Necrotic pulp tissue frequently becomes infected and a proportion of cases of chronic apical periodontitis will result in not only resorption of the periapical bone, but also of apical cementum and dentine (**15A**) and less commonly in lateral root resorption lesions (**15B**).
(ii) Subluxation (avulsion and replantation) ankylosis with replacement resorption.

Lesions of this nature occur most commonly when inappropriate splinting regimes prevent normal physiological movement of the traumatised tooth. This may predispose reorganisation of the blood clot in the periodontal ligament to ankylosis. Typical sites are cervical and apical, and replacement resorption is a frequent complication (**15C**).

(iii) Root fracture.

Mobility of the coronal fragment following transverse root fractures may lead to resorption in the fracture line even though the apical fragment retains its vitality (**15D**).

(iv) Internal resorption may be a late complication when the traumatic injury was of insufficient severity to cause loss of vitality (**15E**).

(b) Chronic force.

Orthodontic forces may lead to root-end resorption. Endodontically treated teeth, and particularly those with lesions of endodontic origin appear to be the most susceptible. The orthodontic forces applied need to be light and interrupted to avoid this complication. Trauma from occlusion is also an occasional cause of root end resorption.

16 This may be caused by a mismatch in the size and shape of the gutta percha point and the file. This may occur at any point along the length of the gutta percha and is coronal to the apical end. The mismatch may be in the diameter at a given level or in the taper and is caused by variations in standardisation of the sizes.

Another reason may be the presence of a ledge in the canal which prevents the passage of the flexible gutta percha point but not of the more rigid file. This lack of rigidity may also prevent the passage of a small size gutta percha point in a canal prepared to an inadequate size. It is usually necessary to prepare to at least a size 25 to the full working length and rarely in severely curved canals to a size 20.

17 The upper right lateral incisor had a root perforation.

Treatment involved the removal of the post retained crown, the cleaning and dressing of the canal space with calcium hydroxide for a period of six weeks, followed by the obturation of the canal with gutta percha and sealant (**17B**). The sinus tract was no longer present when reviewed six months later.

18 This electric pulp tester is turned on automatically when the probe tip touches the tooth and turns off when tooth contact is broken after a 15-second delay. A digital display reads from 0–80 and the only control on the instrument is the rate of increase of the electrical stimulus.

19 (d) Extract the tooth.

20 Even though the acute phase of the abscess may be managed in the short term, the presence of a developmental groove extending the length of the root is likely to present long term problems. The bone loss is related to a palatal periodontal defect which may lead to secondary pulpal involvement. Root canal treatment will not effect a change in the periodontal state of the tooth which has a very poor prognosis.

21 (b) A number of studies have concluded that posts do not strengthen teeth. On the contrary, they weaken teeth, particularly if they are made too thick or too long. Goldman *et al.* (1984) stated 'the primary purpose of a post is to fasten a superstructure to the root, upon which a crown can be fabricated and to which the crown can be cemented. The core or superstructure can be of gold, base metal, amalgam or composite'.

22 (a) The disadvantages cited of amalgam as a root end filling material include:
(i) Corrosion.
(ii) Cannot command set.
(iii) Dimensional change if contaminated by moisture.
(iv) Introduction of mercury based compound into the body.
(v) Scattering of amalgam particles into the tissues which can cause tissue staining.
(vi) Introduction of non-sterile material into the body.
(b)(i) False. In general, leakage studies have shown that amalgam does not provide an effective seal against dye penetration.
(b)(ii) True. In an effort to reduce leakage with amalgam root end fillings, varnish was tested. Studies have shown that varnish does reduce the penetration of dye but it is uncertain whether it is effective in the long term.
(b)(iii) True. Moisture contamination before setting of zinc containing amalgam results in an electrolytic reaction where hydrogen is evolved. The amalgam expands, affecting the seal at the apex.

23 The shortened root is caused by inflammatory root resorption.
The patient admitted a history of trauma to the lower left quadrant. Pulp death and subsequent periapical inflammation can lead to external resorption of the root apex (Goerig and Neaverth, 1991).

24 Whenever a fissure (**24A**) is evident in the floor of the pulp chamber, an additional canal may be expected.
The entrance to the second mesio-buccal canal may be any where along the fissure and a sharp endodontic probe (DG16) will help to feel for the entrance (**24B**).

25 The distal root of the first molar has been replaced through part of its length by sclerotic bone.

Bone sclerosis is often due to low grade inflammatory change. Idiopathic root resorption of vital teeth is sometimes self-limiting and unless some additional factor indicative of continuing inflammatory insult is identified, or there are concomitant symptoms, root canal treatment should be deferred.

The history should be checked for an episode of trauma, including interdental concussive forces, trauma from parafunction or signs and symptoms indicative of tooth fracture. Should examination suggest a vital and asymptomatic pulp, the tooth should be reviewed radiographically until it can be established whether the lesion is progressive before embarking on endodontic treatment.

26 The factors considered include:
(a) Evidence that the original root treatment is failing. There may be symptoms, a sinus tract or a persistent radiolucency.
(b) The need for re-restoring the tooth. If the tooth needs a new restoration it may be an opportune time to replace the root filling.
(c) The recognition of an obvious fault with the root treatment, which may lead to failure.

This particular molar had been symptomful and it was retreated conventionally after removal of the ceramo-metal crown.

27 This scenario may be caused by a number of changes in the root canal and include the following:
(a) A blockage of the apical portion of the canal caused by dentine mud, dislodged pulp stones or restorative material from the coronal restoration.
(b) The development of a ledge short of the working length which prevents negotiation of the file to the full length without careful manipulation of a precurved file.
(c) Alteration of the effective length of the root canal by virtue of inadvertent removal of coronal interferences may give the impression of the file not reaching the full length provided the tip of the file does not bypass the working length.

28) Paste materials may be placed into root canals using one of the following:
(a) A spiral root filler in a slow speed handpiece.
(b) A hand reamer.
(c) An injection system (see **28B**).

A spiral root filler is generally the most effective method but it should only be used if the canal has been enlarged and shaped. A spiral filler should NOT be used if the canal has NOT been enlarged – instead a hand reamer is recommended.

Injection systems are hazardous as the material may be forced into the periapical tissues. Paper points should not be left in canals with a medicament as the paper points can break down and cause periapical inflammation.

29 (a) A history of pain, principally to pressure.
(b) Carious destruction of the marginal ridge of a molar tooth, which in 70% of teeth indicates pulpal involvement.
(c) Radiographic evidence of inter-radicular bone loss associated with a molar tooth, or in the periapical region of a single rooted tooth.
(d) Mobility of the tooth not associated with natural exfoliation.

30 Idiopathic internal resorption. Such lesions may occur in the coronal pulp chamber where they cause 'pink-spot' lesions, if they approach the enamel surface, or they may occur in the root.
Coronal lesions may be misdiagnosed as caries on cursory radiographic examination.

Many such lesions occur in teeth with a history of trauma. Investigation of lesions of this type requires that perforation be identified as early as possible. These teeth usually remain vital. Supra-alveolar perforations may be identified by probing. Sub-alveolar perforations may be identified following extirpation of the pulp using an electronic apex locator which will give atypical results in such circumstances. Root canal treatment is necessary to prevent progression of the destruction.

Particular problems in management include:
(a) A greater than usual dependence on chemical, as opposed to mechanical means of debridement of pulpal debris. Copious irrigation with strong sodium hypochlorite solutions and the use of calcium hydroxide inter-appointment dressings is advocated.
(b) Obturation benefits from the use of a thermoplastic condensation technique. Cold lateral condensation may not be adequate to produce three-dimensional obturation of the space created by such lesions. Suitable techniques would include thermatic compaction, hot vertical plugging or injection of thermo-plasticised gutta percha.
(c) Such teeth may be structurally compromised and careful thought should be given to their restoration.

31 Irreversible pulpitis in the untreated buccal canal of the upper left first premolar. Over 90% of upper first premolars have two separate root canals. The missed canal was responsible for the spontaneous pain which subsided following endodontic treatment of both roots of the premolar.

32 Kilovoltage (kV) controls the penetration of dental X-rays. High kV (90kV) produce shorter wavelength X-rays which are less penetrating and therefore safer to the patient. The radiographic image exhibits increased shades of grey with a longer scale of contrast. Lower kV machines (70kV) produce radiographic images with greater contrast to define radiopaque and radiolucent structures.

Milliamperage (mA) controls the flow of electrons and thus the amount of radiation produced, and it also affects the density and the degree of darkening of the X-ray film.

33 Inflammatory root resorption has lead to the shortening of the distal root of this lower left first molar.

Endodontic therapy in the form of conventional re-treatment will arrest the progress of the inflammatory resorption of the apex of the distal root.

34 There are several classifications that have ben used over the years. Simon *et al.* (1972) divided perio-endo lesions into 5 classes:

Class 1 – Primary endodontic lesions.

Class 2 – Primary endodontic lesions with secondary periodontic involvement.

Class 3 – Primary periodontic lesions.

Class 4 – Primary periodontic lesions with secondary endodontic involvement.

Class 5 – 'True' combined lesions.

This classification has been widely used but recently has been questioned. There are two problems. Firstly, it is difficult to diagnose the difference between the classes and secondly the classification is unnecessarily complicated. In the light of current research a simple classification (Walton and Torabinejad, 1989) based on diagnosis may be more appropriate. Defects are divided into three groups:

Endodontic origin

Periodontic origin (**34A**)

Endo/perio origin (true combined lesions) (**34B**)

A true combined lesion occurs when there is a lesion as a result of a necrotic pulp and there is an independent and concurrent periodontal lesion. **34B** shows a maxillary second molar with periodontal disease and furcation involvement of both molars. In addition the second molar has a deep restoration with a necrotic pulp and an area associated with the distal root apex.

35 ALARA – As Low As Reasonably Achievable.

The principle of ALARA should be followed as closely as possible to reduce the amount of radiation that the patient and the health team receive. This is achieved in the following ways:

(a) The use of high speed film, D (Ultraspeed) or E (Ektaspeed).

(b) Reproducible and meticulous techniques will help reduce the number of necessary radiographs.

(c) Dental X-ray machines should be designed to reduce significantly patient skin dose.

(d) Restriction of the X-ray beam size by collimation using a lead diaphragm within the aiming cone.

(e) Protection of the patient with a lead apron or thyroid collar.

(f) The operator should stand a minimum of 6 feet from the patient and should wear a film badge to register levels of occupational exposure.

36 The presence of a facial fistula may indicate that periradicular suppuration has burrowed its way from the cancellous bone through the cortical plate and finally to the surface of the face.

The source of the infection should be located and eradicated in order to effect resolution of the condition.

Following a full visual dental examination, further investigations involved tracing the sinus tract using a gutta percha cone, taking parallelling radiographs of the mandibular teeth, and performing vitality tests. The source of the infection was identified as a necrotic tooth. Root canal treatment was instituted and healing was evident within 3 weeks (**36B**).

37 (c) Dampened with formocresol and left in place for five minutes.

38 This is known as a C-shaped canal, for obvious reasons, and it seems to be more frequent in people of Asian descent (Yang *et al.*, 1988).

The 'C' may be continuous for the full length of the root or may divide into separate canals in the mid-root. Preparation of this type of canal may be difficult. Files should be drawn around the 'C' during preparation to fully clean the canal system. The use of ultrasonic instrumentation may also be useful. When filling the canal system a combination of warm vertical and cold lateral condensation is required.

39 The affected premolars are evaginated. In this condition, reported more often in patients of Mongoloid origin, a pulp horn extends to the occlusal surface of maxillary and mandibular premolars. It provides the dual complications of pulpal involvement and immature apical development.

Treatment may involve pulpotomy, apexification and root canal therapy.

40 The white line is the lamina dura. It is formed by the tangential passage of the X-ray beam as it crosses the cribriform plate or bone lining the tooth socket. Lack of penetration of the X-rays results in the more opaque radiographic image.

The loss in continuity of the lamina dura is indicative of pathological bony change. This can be the first indication that endodontic treatment or re-treatment is necessary.

41 (c) The pulp tissue of the affected teeth has been replaced by a dentine like material.

42 The instrument is an electronic apex locator.

It has been suggested that these instruments are calibrated to measure the impedance between the oral mucosa and the periodontal ligament at the apical foramen via the root canal. This is supposedly made possible by the fact that the value for this impedance is relatively constant for most root canals. The suggestion that this value is a biological constant is not universally agreed. The same relationship can be derived for a simulated canal in a glass tube *in vitro*.

A number of factors, such as large apical foramina, electrolytes in the canal and contact of one of the electrodes with a metal restoration can cause inaccurate readings. The accuracy of apex locators varies from model to model and between studies using the same model. The range of accuracy of some of the better instruments falls between about 60–90% within 0.5mm of the apical foramen.

43 (c). The presence of an undiagnosed fracture is most likely to be the cause of the discomfort (cracked tooth syndrome). Pain of pulpal origin is characteristically poorly localised. However, inflammation of the pulp alone would not normally give rise to sensitivity to chewing.

This patient was suffering from an undiagnosed fracture of the upper right first molar. On her return, two weeks later, the patient reported fracture of the mesio-palatal cusp of her tooth. At the same time she had noticed relief from the sensitivity to chewing.

44 Root canal sealers lubricate and aid in the sealing of the gutta-percha points. They assist in the filling and sealing of irregularities of the canal walls, patent accessory canals, and multiple foramina. A bacteriostatic action is also desirable.

45 A corticosteroid-antibiotic paste is recommended for 6–8 weeks in an attempt to reduce the inflammatory root resorption. This material acts in two ways: the antibiotic component will reduce the bacterial count in the canal and the tooth root; and the corticosteroid component will reduce the inflammatory response in the periodontal ligament.

46 Once the inflammatory resorption has been arrested, calcium hydroxide should be used as a long term medicament in an attempt to encourage healing with hard tissue at the apex (i.e. apexification). Figure **46** is a radiograph taken at the time of placing the root canal fillings - hard tissue repair of the teeth and the periapical region is evident.

47 (a) It is generally accepted that the length of the post space should be no less than the length of the clinical crown. On the other hand 4–5mm of gutta percha must be left at the apex of the tooth to maintain the apical obturation.

48 The swelling (**48A**) was associated with a lesion of endodontic origin which took the form of an acute periapical abscess involving the upper right first molar. The swelling resolved following root canal treatment of the tooth (**48B, 48C**).

49 External replacement resorption is a common complication of replantation. Replantation is unlikely to succeed in the long term if not attempted within two hours of avulsion. The tooth should not be cleaned but should be stored in an isotonic fluid such as saliva or milk. The socket should not be extensively damaged or severely compromised by periodontal inflammation. The best results are obtained with immature teeth, when vitality may sometimes be recovered. No extra-oral endodontic procedures are usually advisable.

Rigid splinting should be restricted to the acute phase only. A maximum of one week of acid-etch splinting is advisable. If the tooth is mobile and uncomfortable when the splint is removed, a soft non-rigid polyvinyl splint may be provided. Anti-tetanus prophylaxis should be checked and antibiotics prescribed.

Teeth with mature apices should be root treated one to two weeks after replantation. Teeth with open apices may be monitored for revascularisation. Evidence of apical inflammation at three weeks should indicate extirpation and calcium hydroxide therapy to intercept resorption.

50 (c). Cast post and cores offer the least retention, are most likely to lead to tooth fracture should the crown become loose and are the most time consuming to produce. Parallel-sided serrated posts have been shown to be more retentive than the other types cited in the question (Standlee *et al.*, 1978).

51 (a) Leubke–Ochsenbein or submarginal (rectangular) flap.

(b) Preserves gingival margins and does not expose crestal bone.

(c) Severs vertically orientated supraperiosteal vessels; increases the risk of flap shrinkage, delayed healing and scarring.

52 Reasons why these antiseptics are not recommended include:

(a) They are toxic materials.

(b) They cause periapical irritation.

(c) They may have systemic side effects.

(d) Some are mutagenic and/or carcinogenic.

(e) Their antibacterial spectrum of activity is limited.

(f) Their antibacterial action is of short duration.

(g) Their ability to diffuse throughout the entire root canal system in sufficient quantities to produce an antibacterial concentration is doubtful.

53 (d) Internal resorption.

54 The parallelling technique periapical (**54A**) is the most accurate radiograph used in endodontics. The central beam of the X-rays is directed at right angles to the X-ray film and through the apical region of the tooth.

Special devices are available to produce this image with great consistency providing a more accurate estimate of tooth length and the relationship of associated anatomical structures.

In the bisecting angle technique (**54B**) the zygomatic process of the maxilla appears to lie over the palatal root of the upper molar. This hides important information such as a possible lesion of endodontic origin if present at the apex of the palatal root.

The bisecting angle technique is not reproducible and the potential for error causes a great deal of image distortion.

55 There are three reasons for using antibiotics in relation to endodontic treatment:

- As a prophylactic measure for those patients who are at risk of contracting infective endocarditis.
- When there are signs of spreading infection or systemic toxicity.
- When the ideal treatment is not feasible or has not been successful.

56 The differential diagnoses would include traumatic bone cyst, developmental bony defect, periapical cementoma, and early ossifying fibroma. These radiolucent lesions, which may be associated with root apices, do not affect the vitality of the tooth.

An excisional biopsy was performed on the lesion and a definite diagnosis of traumatic bone cyst was made.

57 Vertucci (1978), in his study of 400 mandibular first premolars, found that 30% had more than one root canal and 26% had more than one apical foramen.

There is also evidence to suggest that the prevalence of multiple canals may be higher in negroid and mongoloid populations (Trope *et al.*, 1986; Walker, 1988).

58 Extraction of all four upper incisors and replacement by either a fixed or implant-borne prosthesis. The roots of the incisors have been shortened excessively, and coupled with extensive destruction of tooth tissue by recurrent caries, they are not good candidates for cast post retained restorations.

59 Silver points were first used in a standardised technique where the canals were prepared using a reaming action; the points were selected to match the largest instrument used to prepare the canal to the working length. It is now appreciated that there is a wide discrepancy between the canal wall and the point: a large amount of root canal sealer is required to fill in the space. Sealers tend to dissolve, increasing the chance of leakage. Also, in some instances, silver points can be difficult to remove.

Titanium points have been advocated as an alternative because of their inertness and resistance to corrosion. Gutta percha coated and teflon coated points have also been tested.

Other metal points appear to share many of the disadvantages of silver points.

60 The upper lateral incisor has a Dens Invaginatus (Dens in Dente). During tooth development the enamel is folded into the developing crown. The infolded enamel takes on the appearance of a tooth, hence the 'tooth within a tooth' description.

A pit may be left in the crown of the tooth allowing inflammation and, ultimately, necrosis of the pulp tissue. Infection may travel through the central and peripheral areas of the tooth; both portions have to be cleaned as efficiently as possible. Failure to clean and fill this complex canal system properly will lead to failure. This is why the treatment has appeared to have failed in this case.

If the pit in the crown is sealed as soon as the tooth erupts into the mouth the chances of complications are reduced.

61 Silver point root fillings are commonly associated with extensive external inflammatory resorption. The primary aetiological factor is infection due to inadequate initial debridement or coronal microleakage in the presence of inadequate canal sealing. There is also speculation that corrosion of metallic silver promotes inflammation due to a foreign body type reaction to the toxic corrosion products.

Few root canals are ever approximately circular in cross section, especially after preparation. The silver point sealing technique is heavily dependent on the sealer used. Underfilling is common, which places a particularly strong emphasis on the role of the sealer in any canal which is less than ideally decontaminated during preparation.

Re-treatment (**61B**) depends on the ability to remove the silver points. Ultrasound may be particularly useful in this context. Large volumes of contaminated debris may be lodged adjacent to a failed silver point and meticulous, step-down preparation and cleaning are essential if the frequency of the acute reaction of the removal of the silver point is to be minimised

The apical barrier lost in the resorption process may often be replaced if calcium hydroxide dressings are used for a period of several months.

62 Sometimes, radiographic periapical rarefaction may be visible even when there is vital tissue in the root canals. The periapical bone resorption is probably due to the action of inflammatory mediators draining from the more coronal aspects of the inflamed dental pulp. The lesion is also associated with the sprouting of CGRP-IR (immunoreactive for antibodies to calcitonin gene related peptide) nerve fibres in the periapical tissue. It is believed by some that the release of neuropeptides from these fibres may be responsible for this early periapical lesion (Byers *et al.*, 1990).

63 (c). Use of the coronal-radicular amalgam foundation, with amalgam placed 3–4mm into each canal is now an accepted technique for use in multi-rooted teeth. Nayyar *et al.* (1980) compared amalgam post and cores, with and without full crowns, to cast cores and to natural teeth. They found no difference in compressive strength when the crowns were constructed with a 2mm collar onto sound tooth tissue.

64 Poor wound healing, tendency to scarring, limited access and restricted visibility, and difficult to re-approximate during wound closure (Kramper *et al.*, 1984).

65 (a) A large amalgam restoration with underlying secondary dentine situated over the pulp chamber.
(b) Evidence of an old pulp cap.
(c) Apically, there appears to be an increase in thickness of bony trabeculation (condensing osteitis).
(d) Thickening of the periodontal ligament space and loss of the lamina dura.

66 The presence of a persistent exudate in an instrumented canal may be due to incomplete removal of the pulp, a root fracture, over-instrumentation of the canal and the production of a lateral perforation. In this particular case, there had been a fracture of the mesial root of the lower first molar which allowed seepage of oral fluids into the root canal (**66B**).

67 The Endotec thermal endodontic condenser is a battery operated, heated root canal spreader/plugger. The handpiece consists of a cordless push button heating element with rechargeable batteries. The charger has an AC current converter.
   The heat is used to soften gutta percha into a dense homogeneous mass as part of a warm lateral or vertical condensation technique.

68 Electric pulp test. As with other pulp testing methods, a positive response to the electric pulp test only indicates the presence of a pulpal nerve supply. Its correlation to the integrity of the blood supply and histological condition of the pulp is poor. The reading on the EPT does not indicate the 'degree of health' of the pulpal tissues (Chambers, 1980). Beware of false positive results in partial pulp necrosis and in multi-rooted teeth.

69 After removal of the existing root canal fillings, the canals could be medicated with a corticosteroid-antibiotic paste or a 50:50 mixture of corticosteroid-antibiotic paste and calcium hydroxide for 3–4 weeks to control the symptoms and the infection. Then, long-term calcium hydroxide therapy is indicated to encourage hard tissue repair of the perforation defects.

70 Radiovisiography or the RVG system is a new method of X-ray diagnosis and investigation.
   It features an intra-oral sensor which is fed by an X-ray generator capable of producing a reduction in X-ray exposure by as much as 90% over normal X-ray equipment.
   The instant X-ray image is displayed on a high definition monitor. The image can either be stored on a hard disc or printed as a hard copy image.

71 (d). The full mucoperiosteal rectangular flap provides maximum access and visibility.

72 Second canals in lower second premolars may occur with a frequency of 10% (Zillich and Dowson, 1973).

73 The film shows a large radiolucent lesion in the left maxillary region and suggests that the teeth may have drifted. The size and extent of the lesion, and the nature of its periphery are better shown by an occlusal film (**73B**). An indication of the pathological process involved may be given by aspiration biopsy prior to surgical enucleation.

The lesion proved to be a calcifying odontogenic cyst rather than an odontogenic keratocyst. Cysts and tumours of epithelial origin are the most likely to be associated with pressure resorption although cysts are far more commonly associated with displacement of teeth. In this case, the judgement was that enucleation would lead to the loss of vitality of several teeth; interceptive endodontic treatment was prescribed (**73C**).

74 (a) is false.

75 The most important aim of root canal therapy is to reduce the bacterial contamination of the root canal system to a minimum, such that the balance of activity between the bacteria and the host defences is tipped in favour of the latter to allow healing (Klevant and Eggink, 1983).

76 Direct trauma has resulted in a transverse fracture of the middle third of the root. The coronal fragment has a degree of mobility incompatible with calcific barrier healing and there has been fibrous union. Ultimately, the vitality of the coronal fragment was compromised and external inflammatory resorption in the fracture line was initiated. There is no evidence to suggest loss of vitality of the apical fragment. At this stage, the most conservative option was to initiate treatment with calcium hydroxide therapy to the coronal fragment. Subsequently, endodontic treatment to the calcific barrier, induced above the fracture line may, maintain the tooth.

The preferred management, had the patient presented immediately following the trauma, would have involved splinting and occlusal adjustment with the object of maintaining the vitality of both fragments and of achieving calcific repair.

77 The three zones of histological changes in response to formocresol are, moving apically: (a) fixation, (b) coagulative necrosis and (c) normal vital tissue.

After three days the zone adjacent to the formalized zinc oxide dressing shows no signs of cellular activity because the cells have undergone fixation.

The middle zone contains cells with minimum microscopic detail and are in a state of coagulative necrosis.

In the apical zone the tissue appears to be vital. This could be normal vital radicular pulp tissue, or possibly an ingrowth of reparative granulation tissue. Given time all of the radicular tissue can be replaced by reparative granulation tissue.

78 In common with most teeth, this lateral incisor has lateral canals found mainly in the apical third of the root (**78B**).

Lateral canals are extremely difficult to detect radiographically, although areas of bone loss adjacent to a lateral canal may be seen.

No special techniques have been developed for cleaning or filling lateral canals. Thorough preparation and cleaning of the main root canal using normal methods will allow some cleansing of lateral canals. Filling the canal with sealer and lateral or warm vertical condensation of gutta percha will in many instances fill these lateral canals.

79 The tooth was endodontically treated to the level of the transverse root fracture. Since there is an open end to the canal at the fracture line, long term calcium hydroxide is recommended to encourage the development of a hard tissue barrier at the fractured end of the canal. This will enable the eventual placement of a root canal filling in the coronal fragment. **79B** is a three year follow-up of this tooth.

Note: The pulp in the apical fragment normally remains vital and hence it should not require endodontic treatment.

80 (b) As well as corrosion problems, non-noble alloys are environmentally hazardous to clinicians and technicians if ground particles are inhaled. The palladium derived alloys are low in cost, safe and strong. Gold alloys can be used but are not as strong.

81 The three instruments from left to right are the Canal Master, the Flexogate, and the Gates–Glidden.

All three instruments have a non-cutting pilot tip and a parallel-sided shank of round cross-section which is narrower than the cutting tip. The instruments have a rotary cutting action.

The Gates-Glidden is used in a rotary handpiece to enlarge the coronal portion to the root canal. The Canal Master and Flexogate hand instruments are designed to be used by hand in the preparation of the apical portion of the root canal.

82 A size 20 gutta percha point has been placed into a chronic draining sinus which was evident clinically between the two upper premolar teeth.

The clinical location of the sinus tract would lead one to suspect that there was a problem with one of the two premolar teeth. The point indicates that the source of the chronic draining sinus is in fact the mesio-buccal root of the first molar, which requires re-treatment.

83 Calm reassurance is necessary to gain the mother's confidence and help. If possible the tooth should be replaced without delay into the socket. If the tooth is dirty it should be rinsed gently with cold tap water; no attempt should be made to scrub the tooth or apply antiseptics. If it is not possible to replace the tooth it should be put into a glass of milk. If milk is not available the tooth can be held in the buccal sulcus of the patient. The tooth must not be allowed to dry out.

The tooth should be replanted, after proper rinsing, as soon as the patient arrives at the dental office. An arch wire splint retained with resin on etched enamel should be placed for 10 days. When the splint is removed the canal is cleaned, prepared and calcium hydroxide placed and the access cavity sealed. The tooth is observed at 3-monthly intervals and the calcium hydroxide replaced as required. At one year the root canal is filled with gutta percha.

In teeth with open apices the pulp may revascularise provided the time between avulsion and replantation was less than 2 hours. In these cases it may not be necessary to carry out root treatment. The tooth is reviewed at 3-monthly intervals.

84 This is a form of wedge test to detect a cracked tooth. The wedge in use is a bi-convex rubber polishing disc. This may be used instead of the more traditional methods of creating a wedging effect e.g. golf tee or mirror handle.

85 This autoclavable syringe is capable of extruding gutta percha at a temperature of 70°C.

Prefilled disposable cannulae, containing gutta percha with 22 gauge stainless steel needles, are heated in a portable heating unit, and then inserted into the syringe. The trigger is squeezed to express the plasticised gutta percha. The technique is used with a suitable root canal sealer and the soft gutta percha is condensed using root canal pluggers.

86 Pain which cannot be located and reacts to hot and cold is invariably due to pulpitis. In this case the inflammatory process is still confined to the pulp space, in the later stages toxins will pass through the apical foramina and initiate an inflammatory response from the vessels in the periodontal ligament. The tooth will then become tender to touch.

The treatment will depend on the operator's diagnosis as to whether the pulp has been irreversibly damaged or not. Clinical signs and symptoms cannot be related to pulpal histology so the decision by the operator is empirical. It is generally agreed that the pulp is likely to be irreversibly damaged if the pain is constant, that hot or cold stimulates the pain which then lasts for several minutes or longer, and finally that the pain is worse at night. In this case the pulp would appear to be irreversibly damaged so root canal treatment should be undertaken.

87 There appears to be almost complete healing of the lesion around the mesial root whilst the lesion associated with the distal root has completely healed.

The possibility that the second molar tooth is also involved is quite clearly repudiated.

88 (b) or (d).

(a) It is wrong to place amalgam directly over a pulp stump as the remaining pulp will become necrotic. It would be equivalent to placing amalgam directly over a traumatic pulpal exposure in a restorative cavity.

(b) Leaving the pulp stump exposed is recommended as the patient does not have any discomfort (Tagger and Smukler, 1977). If left, the pulp will gradually become necrotic so the tooth must be root filled 10–14 days later.

(c) Root canal treatment is always required when a root with a vital pulp is resected.

(d) If it is known which root is to be resected beforehand then the tooth can be root filled. A suitable restoration, such as amalgam, may be placed in the straight part of the root which is to be resected.

89 (a) The formocresol is capable of producing mummification, disinfection and analgesia. It is effective against vegetative bacteria, fungi and even some viruses. However, it is only mildly effective against sporing and acid fast bacteria. Formocresol is most effective under conditions of high humidity because in order to react with the protein of a micro-organism it must be in solution.

(b) Tricresol, which is a disinfectant which is based upon the phenol molecule, when in a solution of 0.3–0.6% will destroy Gram positive and Gram negative bacteria within ten minutes. Further it is less effective against bacterial spores and its efficacy is adversely affected by proteinaceous materials such as blood. The phenol molecule has the ability to paralyse sensory nerve endings; hence, tricresol has analgesic properties.

(c) Glycerine is used to increase the viscosity of the solution and to reduce the caustic nature of the tricresol.

90 Lateral root perforation. A careful tracing of the mesial surface of the distal root suggests that the root surface is concave. A cylindrical post is liable to cause a perforation in this 'danger zone'. The presence of a perforation was confirmed after the removal of the post using ultrasonic vibration.

91 One of the difficulties in root canal therapy has been the preparation of curved root canals to meet the ideal of a regular taper with minimum diameter at the apical constriction and maximum at the coronal end, without altering the curvature of the canal significantly. The use of rigid instruments in unskilled and sometimes skilled hands can result in zipping in the apical portion of the canal and excessive dentine removal on the inner aspect of the curve. In addition to the potential for perforation, this leads to a canal shape which has a minimal diameter some distance away from the constriction, making it difficult to obturate the apical portion of the canal satisfactorily.

The rationale for the more flexible and safe-ended instruments is that they would reduce the potential preferential removal of dentine on particular aspects of the canal and therefore produce prepared canals which follow the curvature of the original canal and root more closely.

92 It is very common for upper premolars to exhibit two roots or one root with two root canals.

In the case demonstrated, only one of the two canals has been cleaned and toxins are leaking out into the periapical tissues from the unprepared and unfilled canal. This accounts for the continuing symptoms and the persistent periapical lesion.

Alteration of the angle of the X-ray beam by adopting a mesial approach reveals the presence of two canals (**92B**).

Diagnostic working lengths and final X-rays should be taken using a cone angulation technique (buccal object rule).

93 (d) Removing broken posts can be a perilous occupation. Pliers can often lead to tooth fracture, while attempts to drill out posts are time consuming, frustrating and often end in disaster. Using a large ultrasonic scaler carries little risk and is often effective. Should removal not be forthcoming, it may be wiser to attempt to build up the core with composite rather than run the risk of tooth fracture.

94 The cemented band provides coronal support during the endodontic phase of treatment. Heat should be used to plasticise the gutta percha so as not to induce excessive pressure during canal obturation.

Providing the root canal treatment can be completed satisfactorily, the pulp chamber should be sealed using a material with dentine bonding and sealing qualities prior to providing an occlusally protective coronal restoration. In this situation post retained restorations should be avoided.

95 These gutta percha condensers use the principle of the reverse-turning screw. They are capable of softening gutta percha by friction, and compacting it ahead of and lateral to the rotating shaft. The process is known as thermomechanical compaction.

The instrument heats and softens the gutta percha, which is pushed ahead of the shaft of the instrument, forcing the compactor to withdraw from the canal.

Without the presence of a good apical stop, it is possible to overfill the root canal. This can be avoided by using the 'hybrid' technique (Tagger *et al.*, 1984), where the bulk of the canal is first laterally condensed and then the obturation is enhanced by thermomechanical compaction.

96 Incision and drainage are carried out to release haemorrhagic or purulent exudate that is entrapped within the tissue and cannot be drained through the canal. The swelling should not be incised unless it is localised and fluctuant.

Anaesthesia should be obtained avoiding injection into inflamed tissue, regional block anaesthesia may be required. The incision should be made firmly down onto bone. A drain is not normally required. The tooth should be isolated and the root canals prepared. Antibiotics are unnecessary unless there are systemic effects.

97 Atypical facial pain. The management includes a full history of the pain and of any emotional disturbances such as anxiety or depression. Every care should be taken to exclude latent carious lesions, cracked teeth, and other pulpal pathology during the clinical examination. If the diagnosis of atypical facial pain is made, the nature of the pain is discussed with the patient. Medication such as tricyclic antidepressants or mono-amine-oxidase inhibitors may be prescribed after consultation with an expert in facial pain and/or a psychiatrist (Rees and Harris, 1978–79).

98 Inflammatory resorption may be slowed or arrested. Replacement resorption is unlikely to respond to treatment.

The root canal should be thoroughly prepared, cleaned and disinfected. The tooth may be provisionally dressed with calcium hydroxide for a 6–12 month period prior to permanently obturating the canal.

It is important to realise that root resorption, although presenting unfavourable radiographic appearances, is not incompatible with the survival of teeth for relatively long periods.

99 DIAGNOSIS
(a) To identify pathological changes within the pulp, periapical tissues and periodontium.
(b) To study pulp and root anatomy, the location and number of roots and root canals and their degree of curvature.
(c) To differentiate between pathologic and non-pathologic and anatomical structures that lie in close proximity to or are superimposed over roots.
TREATMENT
(a) To determine working length.
(b) To determine the number of canals present.
(c) To assist the placement of the master filling point.
(d) To evaluate the quality of obturation.
RECALL
Radiographs are essential to assess the success or failure of endodontic treatment over a given time period.

100 (b) 'Conventional wisdom' used to hold that posts reinforce teeth weakened by the loss of vitality. Numerous studies have shown that posts weaken teeth and therefore the first option is unnecessary and even counterproductive. Crowning lower incisors is fraught with problems including risk of perforation, tooth fracture, poor aesthetics and so on. As the crown of the tooth is intact, non-vital bleaching is the most favoured option. Should the discolouration still be a problem after bleaching, a veneer is usually preferable to crowning.

101 All of these cavity designs have been used or suggested. The choice of cavity design is dependent on the individual case. All the different designs have been advocated.

102 The buccal object rule enables the clinician when taking radiographs to separate and identify structures that are facially and lingually placed.

When the projection angle of the X-ray tube is changed, the structure or object closest to the buccal will appear to move in the opposite direction to that which the X-ray cone moves.

Working length radiographs are dependent on this technique when buccal and lingual canals of the same tooth would otherwise be superimposed.

This working length radiograph of a lower molar (**102A**) has been taken with the tube head at 30 degrees from the mesial (**102B**). The buccal canal is more distally placed in relation to the lingual canal.

103 This patient is suffering from pericoronitis associated with the partial eruption of the lower right third molar. Insertion of a gutta percha point into the sinus indicates the origin of the infection (**103B**).

104 There are two important pieces of information you would require:
(a) The presence of any periodontal pockets in the furcation area and the nature of these pockets. A deep isolated pocket may be a drainage track for an endodontic lesion, whereas pocketing that is more widespread in nature would indicate a periodontal infection.
(b) The quality of the root filling. In this case two canals had been missed completely and the other two canals had not been treated properly. Following re-treatment the inter-radicular lesion resolved (**104B**).

More than a quarter of lower first molars have two distal canals (Skidmore and Bjorndal, 1971)

105 (d) is the correct answer. There is evidence to suggest that closing a tooth after drainage and cleaning the root canal(s) and not leaving it open will reduce the number of appointments and the frequency of exacerbations (Weine *et al.*, 1975). If the drainage cannot be stopped, which is rare, the tooth is left open for 24 hours and then cleaned and closed. Leaving a tooth open to drain allows micro-organisms to pass into the canal system from the oral cavity and the results may be difficult to treat.

106 (d) Use of vaseline, rubber dam and waxed floss ligatures is mandatory to protect the gingival tissues from caustic levels (30–35%) of hydrogen peroxide commonly used. By protecting the gingivae and using such concentrations the treatment can be reduced. In less severe cases it may be possible to reduce the concentration of the bleaching agent used.

107 Most gutta percha points contain the following ingredients although the proportions in different brands may vary; gutta percha, zinc oxide, barium sulphate, waxes, resins and colouring agents. The largest component is zinc oxide followed by gutta percha which is usually about 20%.

108 The important anatomical features, from the top, are:

    Narrow occlusal table

    Thin enamel

    Large pulp horns

    Bulbous crown

    Enamel prism inclination

    Cervical constriction

    Thin pulpal floor

    Fine ribbon-shaped canals

    Developing permanent tooth

The thin enamel means that the progression of caries can be rapid.

Secondary dentine deposits in the pulp chamber, can make the locating of the pulp horns difficult, so that when attempting to locate the pulp horn they may be inadvertently mistaken for the entrances of the root canals; resulting in a perforation of the pulp chamber.

The thin pulpal floor can be easily penetrated by a rotary instrument; which may cause damage to the permanent successor tooth.

The ribbon-like root canals cannot be easily cleaned by mechanical means; this process is further hampered by the curvature of the roots which can be perforated if mechanical cleansing is attempted.

The cervical constriction favours the fitting of a stainless steel crown as the final restoration.

109 This is a surgical bony defect. A detailed history revealed that the patient had endodontic treatment and periapical surgery performed on his upper right lateral incisor before it had been removed. The presence of scattered particles of amalgam in the radiolucent area also serve to indicate previous periapical surgery. A bony defect was diagnosed clinically using bi-manual palpation of the area.

110 An incisally adjusted access cavity facilitates the location and straight line negotiation of both buccal and lingual canals.

111 Corticosteroid-antibiotic paste could be used as an inter-appointment medicament to reduce inflammation in the periapical tissues via the action of the corticosteroid component, triamcinolone.

Note that the foramen of the distal canal (**111B**) is to the distal of the root and the tooth was temporised with a stainless steel band and a reinforced glass ionomer cement during the endodontic treatment.

112 In curved roots of molars, preparation of the canal which straightens the curve, risks perforating the canal towards the furcation. This can be avoided by directing instrumentation towards the safety zone or the bulky part of the root (**112B**). Elimination of undercuts in the access cavity will aid preparation of the canals towards the bulky part of the root.

Treatment of strip perforations are difficult and often end in the removal of a root or the whole tooth.

113 Placement of a rubber dam clamp may also be facilitated by a stainless steel crown, an orthodontic band, a pin retained amalgam or composite restoration.

114 Non-intervention. The coronal fragment of the upper left central incisor was firm and responded to pulp tests. Apical fragments, following root fractures, usually remain vital and do not require removal (Andreasen and Andreasen, 1990).

115 No active treatment is required other than long term observation.

Although the extrusion of the iodoform paste through the apex is not ideal, in a few months the excess paste will resorb.

116 (a) Lignocaine hydrochloride 2% with 1:50,000 adrenaline is the optimum. Adrenaline is a better vasoconstrictor than Felypressin but at concentrations of 1:80,000 and 1:100,000 it does not provide sufficient vasoconstriction for surgical purposes.

117 A number of different measures may help:
(a) Use precurved files, the curvature of which matches that of the canal as far as possible in gauge clinically.
(b) Use more flexible files to maintain the original curvature during filing.
(c) Use the smaller sized files to carry out most of the instrumentation and do not force the larger sized files to the working length.
(d) The progressive shaping of the canal to increase its size can be controlled more effectively by the use of intermediate sized files created by cutting the tips of the smaller files.
(e) The part of the file likely to remove dentine in an uncontrolled manner can be modified by the removal of the flutes with a diamond nail file. This usually involves the outer aspect of the apical portion. Alternatively instruments designed for the purpose e.g. Canal Master may be selected.
(f) Excessive removal of dentine from the inner aspect of the curve of the canal can be avoided by the use of anticurvature filing. This simply means that fewer strokes of the file are employed on the inner curve than around the remainder of the circumference of the canal (Abou-Rass *et al.*, 1980).

118 Root canals should be prepared and obturated to the apical constriction. This is the narrowest portion of the root canal situated just inside the dentine-cement junction (**118B**).

When a canal is prepared to the so-called radiographic apex, preparation often extends beyond the apical constriction and into the apical periodontal tissues.

119 Three main reasons for failure to heal may be advanced:
(a) It is most likely that the lesion is not healing. Residual infection may remain in the root canal system because of inadequate instrumentation or a complex canal anatomy. Certain types of micro-organism are more resistant to remove, i.e. pseudomonas. In a number of rare instances the infection may become established outside the root canal system, either in the periapical tissue or on the external root surface and healing is therefore hindered.

In some cases the formation of a cyst within a granuloma not associated with the periapex of the tooth may remain and continue to grow even after conventional root canal therapy.

The response of the host in healing is also important. Systemic factors which are as yet poorly defined can slow down the normal healing mechanisms. In more specific circumstances, the presence of foreign bodies in the periapical tissues could contribute to the formation of a giant cell lesion which remains as a radiolucent area.

Whenever there is a periapical lesion present it is important to allow time for the lesion to heal.
(b) In some cases, although the infection is eliminated and there is absence of inflammation, healing occurs by fibrous tissue formation which gives the appearance of a radiolucent lesion. In rare instances the cortical bone may fail to regenerate, despite adequate periapical bone healing giving the appearance of a periapical area.
(c) The persistence of a periapical lesion may also signify misdiagnosis. Both normal anatomic structures, e.g. mental foramen and non-dental pathology can give the appearance of a periapical lesion.

120 In the lower first and second premolar region the mental foramen is often mistaken for a lesion of endodontic origin at the root apex. If a radiograph is taken from another angle the anatomical structure will move in relation to the root apex.

121 The cause of the pain is an acute apical abscess. It is a typical feature that once the cortical plate has been breached and a swelling appears the pain subsides. The tooth is usually extruded from its socket.

The treatment is to remove the cause of the abscess which is the micro-organisms and their toxins lying within the root canal system. Block anaesthesia is given, rubber dam applied and an access cavity cut. The pulp chamber is cleaned using copious amounts of sodium hypochlorite solution. The canal entrances are located and a fine instrument inserted into the straight part of each canal until resistance is felt, the canals are filed to this level. Sodium hypochlorite is used with a gauge 27 needle and syringe. When the straight part of the canal has been opened, a Gates–Glidden no. 2 then 3 is used to widen the coronal portion of the canals. The lengths of each canal are then determined with a diagnostic radiograph. The apical few millimetres are prepared with files and the canals are cleaned with the irrigant. Calcium hydroxide paste is placed in the canals using a spiral root canal filler or contra-rotating a small file. Cotton wool is placed in the pulp chamber and the access cavity is sealed with a temporary dressing. The patient is given analgesics.

122 Amalgam tattoo. Apicectomies have been attempted on the upper incisors on two separate occasions. A history of apical surgery is also suggested by the presence of scarring in the attached gingivae.

123 The sudden disappearance of the canal indicates a bifurcation (or trifurcation) of the canal into buccal and lingual components. This can often be a difficult endodontic case to treat.

124 Any misused root canal instrument can fracture, and certain instruments are more susceptible. This is related to the way in which they are manufactured and the manner in which they are used.

A number of instruments have their cutting flutes machined into the shank whereas others are twisted. The machined variety are more prone to fracture and include such files as Hedstroem and Flex-R. Other instruments may be more susceptible to fracture because of the properties of the metal used and its diameter in cross-section. The initial version of the narrow shanked Canal Master instruments may have fallen into this category. The mode of use of the instruments can increase the chance of fracture. For example, Hedstroem files are designed to be used in a push-pull filing motion and if the instrument is screwed into the canal in a rotary movement, the accumulation of stresses in the machined flutes could result in fracture.

125 The fracture in the maxillary premolar may have been undiagnosed and existed prior to the root canal treatment or restoration of the tooth.

The most significant event in the dental history appears to be the provision of the crown, which would seem to indicate that the placement of the post retained amalgam core led to a fracture and the leakage which ultimately resulted in the loss of the tooth.

The corrosion products are probably derived from the silver contained in the sealant used during the root canal treatment.

126 (a) True.
(b) True.
(c) True.
(d) False.
(e) True.

127 One would suspect a radicular cyst or neoplastic lesion. A chronic periapical abscess would not normally cause an expansion of the cortical plate.

The lesion was biopsied and diagnosed as Hodgkin's lymphoma.

128 The surgical flap should be designed so that:
(a) There is an adequate blood supply.
(b) The flap edge lies on sound bone.
(c) The flap is of a suitable size and is cleanly reflected with minimal trauma.
(d) Sharp angles are avoided.
(e) The integrity of the interdental papilla is maintained.
(f) The incision goes through the periosteum.
(g) There is minimal disruption to the vascular supply and soft tissue attachments.

129 The canal should be thoroughly biomechanically cleaned and shaped with copious sodium hypochlorite irrigation. Then calcium hydroxide paste should be used as an intracanal medicament to necrotise tissue at the resorption site and to ensure removal of all debris from the resorptive defect. The calcium hydroxide should also aid the periodontal healing if there are any perforations present. Several dressings with calcium hydroxide at 2–3 weekly intervals are usually required.

Note: if there had been pain present prior to treatment then an initial intracanal dressing of corticosteroid-antibiotic paste could have been utilised.

130 Intra-oral palpation assists in determining the presence of incipient swelling in relation to the root apices of teeth, and helps corroborate tender areas on the face. It also provides important information with regard to the need for incisional drainage.

131 After a vital pulp extirpation the periodontal ligament may become inflamed for 24–36 hours producing mild symptoms.

The temporary restoration is high.

Vital pulp tissue remains in a canal or an additional canal has not been found.

Necrotic and/or infected debris have been extruded through the apex.

Intracanal medication has been used which is irritating the periapical tissues.

The tooth is fractured.

132 If the teeth are extruded and the patient is seen soon after the injury, the teeth can be repositioned, the occlusion can be checked, and the teeth can be splinted for 2–3 weeks.

The exposed dentine on the fractured crown should be protected with calcium hydroxide.

The endodontic status of the teeth can be evaluated at 6–8 weeks.

If treatment of the teeth is delayed there is a possibility of root resorption, loss of periodontal support, and it may be necessary to reposition the teeth orthodontically after healing has occurred.

133 The root resorption has been caused by orthodontic movement of the teeth. The patient received orthodontic treatment to retrocline the upper incisor teeth some years ago.

No treatment is required unless there is evidence of irreversible pulpal change and loss of vitality of the teeth.

134 No. Although the patient did not report any symptoms the radiographic evidence suggests that the treatment has failed.

The inter-radicular radiolucency appears to have well defined margins and could be a furcation granuloma with an epithelium. Alternatively, it may be a cystic lesion; such lesions have been reported following pulpotomies with formocresol and other phenol containing compounds. The pathology may have been present, but undetected, prior to the original pulpotomy.

135 Ultrasound has been recommended for canal preparation. It can be a very efficient means of irrigating root canal systems, particularly those which are irregular in shape and are unlikely to be properly instrumented by mechanical means alone. This efficacy is especially marked when used with sodium hypochlorite.

Unfortunately, ultrasonically aided canal shaping has not proved to be a very controlled way of achieving the desired shape. The ability to do so varies from machine to machine.

It has also been suggested that application of sealer to the canal walls can be carried out rapidly and effectively using an ultrasonically energised file. However, it is important to use a sealer whose setting is not accelerated by the heat generated with this method.

Ultrasonically activated spreaders have been shown to be an effective means of plasticising gutta percha during lateral condensation. The potential for generating excessive heat should be borne in mind in order to avoid damage to the periodontal ligament.

Ultrasonic activation of specially developed instruments have been suggested as an effective means of preparing retrograde cavities during periapical surgery.

136 Those of periodontic origin. By the time a periodontic lesion can be mistaken for an endodontic lesion, because of the pattern of bone loss, the periodontal disease is advanced. Periodontal breakdown will eventually lead to pulpal necrosis when the apical foramina become involved. By this time the tooth will become mobile and the prognosis hopeless.

137 Long-term use of a 50:50 mixture of corticosteroid-antibiotic paste and a calcium hydroxide paste has been recommended for the treatment of large radiolucent lesions. Alternatively, a calcium hydroxide paste could be used alone. If this conservative approach does not result in healing, then surgery should be considered. This particular case was treated with corticosteroid-antibiotic paste and calcium hydroxide for six months followed by calcium hydroxide paste alone for a further six months. **137B** is a radiograph of this tooth three years after the new root canal filling was placed. Considerable periapical bone repair and an apical hard tissue barrier are evident.

138 The three instruments, from left to right are, a Hedstroem file, a K-type file, and a K-type reamer.

The routine use of K-type reamers in canal preparation has diminished. Reamers are used to enlarge and shape canals into a round cross-section using a turning action. No root canal is round in cross-section nor can it be prepared to a round cross-section either.

The main action in preparing root canals involves the rasping or filing of the canal walls. K-type reamers do not lend themselves to this action.

139 Reduce blood flow at injected site.

Decrease absorption rate of anaesthetic agent into the systemic circulation.
Decrease the potential for toxic reactions to the anaesthetic agent.
Prolong the period of anaesthesia.

140 Conventional root canal treatment is the first line of treatment in nearly all cases of periapical radiolucent lesions (Wood *et al.*, 1980). If conventional endodontic treatment fails to bring about signs of healing in 3–6 months, surgical intervention is indicated.

In this case, near complete resolution of the radiolucent area was attained about one year after root canal treatment of the upper left central and lateral incisors (**140C**).

(Radiographs courtesy of Dr. Alex Chan, Postgraduate Dental Officer in Conservative Dentistry, The Prince Philip Dental Hospital, Hong Kong)

141 (a) False. The main purpose of sutures is to maintain the approximation of the wound edges. Once healing has progressed to a point when artificial stabilisation is no longer required, sutures should be removed. As healing following endodontic surgery is usually rapid, it is unnecessary to delay suture removal. Therefore, sutures can be removed as early as 48 hours after surgery and certainly leaving them for a week is counter-productive.
(b) True.
(c) True. There are two standards for classifying non-absorbable suture sizes, the USP (US Pharmacopoeia) and the EP (European Pharmacopoeia) standard.
(d) True. The suture material is derived from the submucosa or serosa of sheep or bovine intestines.

142 (a) If a round steel bur is used to clean out the contents of the pulp chamber it should be large in size (no. 6 or 8), and be run slowly in a reverse direction.

(b) A perforation of the floor of the pulp chamber can be indicated by the persistent oozing of blood from the floor of the pulp chamber, which may have been mistaken for inadequately amputated, or hyperaemic radicular pulp tissue. The presence, in the centre of the pulpal floor of an area which is harder to the explorer than the sides of the pulp chamber is likely to be the crown of the developing premolar (**142B**).

143 An abrupt change in the density of a root canal indicates bifurcation. The septum of dentine between the buccal and lingual canals has contributed to the calcification-like appearance in the root. Bifurcation of the neighbouring tooth, the lower right central incisor can also be seen on the same radiograph.

Up to 40% of lower incisors have bifurcated root canals although most of them merge to form a single apical foramen.

144 As one searches for the root canal a radiograph (**144B**) can be taken with the bur placed in the access cavity to assess the depth and alignment along the long axis of the tooth. If necessary, more than one radiograph taken at different horizontal angulations can be used to establish the position of the bur.

Subsequent radiographs are taken to assess the working length when once the canal is located.

145 (b) The straight fissure bur produces a relatively smooth surface. A grooved surface is produced by both the cross-cut fissure and the round bur as it gouges dentine. The diamond bur produces a fine rippled surface (Nedderman *et al.*, 1988).

146 One of the most important principles of access cavity preparation is to provide straight line access to as much of the root canal system as possible. This can be compromised in a number of ways including:
(a) Lack of removal of the entire roof of the pulp chamber.
(b) Incorrect siting of the access cavity within the crown.
(c) The cavity may be too small or have the wrong shape.

147 Calcium hydroxide should be used as a long term medicament in order to encourage the development of an apical hard tissue barrier (i.e. apexification) prior to placing the final root canal filling. A calcium hydroxide paste was used in this tooth for 18 months and **147B** shows the tooth three years after the root canal filling was placed. An apical hard tissue barrier is evident.

148 The two mesially placed lesions are of external resorption. This is confirmed by the visible outline of the root canal through the defect.
The distal defect is internal resorption which in this instance appears as a radiographically enlarged root canal space.

149 (d) A traumatic injury to this tooth, which cannot be remembered.

150 (a) False. After root end resection, if the seal at the apex is judged to be adequate, there is no necessity to place a root end filling.
(b) False. Bevelling the root surface actually removes more root than a straight horizontal resection. The primary reason for bevelling is to improve access and visibility.
(c) True. A surgical approach is not a panacea for treating endodontic problems. When problems prevent thorough cleaning, adequate shaping and complete filling of the root canal, a surgical approach may be necessary. Surgical endodontics has not been shown to have a predictably higher success rate than conventional non-surgical endodontic treatment.
(d) False. A tooth with a fractured or broken instrument in the root canal should be treated conventionally in the first instance. Attempts should be made to remove the fractured instrument whenever feasible. If this proves unsuccessful, the canal should be cleaned, shaped and filled to the level of the retained instrument. The tooth should then be monitored and surgical treatment is only needed when there are signs or symptoms of failure. Studies indicate that the prognosis of teeth treated by this approach is good (Grossman, 1968; Crump and Natkin, 1970; Fox *et al.*, 1972).
(e) False. When possible, the post should be removed and conventional root canal treatment instituted. It is pointless carrying out surgery in the hope of 'bottling up' the bacteria within the root canal because, unless the reservoir of bacteria in the main canal is eliminated, it will continue to feed the periradicular infection. In addition, conventional treatment by post removal is more conservative and does not reduce the length of the root.

151 (a) Poor oral hygiene.
(b) Poor bony support for the tooth.
(c) Fused roots.
(d) Short thin roots.
(e) Deep furcation requiring considerable destruction of supporting bone in order to resect the root.
(f) Anatomy that precludes the formation of a functional band of attached gingivae around the remaining roots.

152 Barbed broaches are made from soft steel wire of varying thickness. The barbs are formed by cutting into the metal and forcing the cut portion away from the shaft so that the tip of the barb points towards the handle. The cuts are made eccentrically around the shaft so as not to weaken it.

They can also be used to remove gross debris, necrotic tissue and cotton wool dressings.

153 There are two separate distal roots in this lower molar and the immediate post operative radiograph illustrates this (**153B**). On the preoperative radiograph (**153A**) the periodontal ligament space over the distal roots can be followed showing two distinct outlines.

Apical root resorption of the disto-buccal root is the other feature evident on the radiograph. The resorption has altered the normal anatomy of the apex, causing loss of the apical constriction. Over-preparation and over-filling may occur as a result and a definite apical stop in sound dentine must be established.

154 A commonly accepted guideline is to prepare the apical part of the canal to three sizes larger than the first file that binds at the apical extent of the canal. This guideline is modified to prevent procedural errors, such as ledging, zipping and perforation, by stipulating a maximum size such as 25 or 30 for curved or narrow canals. The selection of these guidelines is empirical and is based on the fact that it seems to provide acceptable results clinically.

155 (e) A stainless steel crown at this appointment.

156 The large radiolucency is a unilateral palatal cleft. The condition can be readily diagnosed clinically. This case illustrates the importance of not spot diagnosing conditions using radiographs alone. Radiographs are an adjunct to, not a substitute for, clinical examination.

157 Most of the problems of this method of canal preparation are related to the fact that the apical part of the canal is prepared to its final shape first and the rest of the canal is prepared subsequently. As the coronal part of the canal is not cleaned prior to the placement of files to the full working length, the risk of extruding debris through the apical foramen is relatively high. The lack of initial coronal preparation also means that in the early part of the preparation it is often not possible to place the irrigation needle sufficiently far into the root canal to achieve satisfactory apical debridement. This can encourage the formation of dentine mud and the blockage of canals. This is the main reason for instrument recapitulation.

Although the aim of the technique is to prepare the apical part of the canal first, the presence of flutes along most of the length of the file results in simultaneous removal of dentine more coronally, particularly in curved canals. This can result in alteration of the effective working length as the instrumentation progresses.

In order to overcome these problems, the step-down method of canal preparation has gained favour.

158 This swelling is a mucous retention cyst or a mucocoele. There is usually no sign of inflammation or lymphadenopathy associated with the condition.

159 There appears to be a space between the canal wall and the root canal filling in the distal canal.

This is indicative of a fractured root which 'pinches' the periodontal ligament tissues when biting pressure is relieved.

160 This has been achieved in three ways:
(a) By changing the geometry of the cross-section of the shank from that of a square or rhomboidal shape to a triangle.
(b) By confining the flutes on the instrument to the apical portion and reducing the diameter of the remainder of the shank.
(c) By changing the metallic alloy of which the files are made to one with greater resilience, such as titanium or nickel titanium.

161 The existing root canal filling was removed so that the canal could be re-treated. Since there was an 'open apex', it was necessary to do apexification (using long-term calcium hydroxide) on this tooth prior to placing a new root canal filling. Finally, after the new root filling had been completed, the tooth was internally bleached. Figs.**161C, 161D** show the new root canal filling and the tooth six months after treatment.

162 A cast restoration would not normally be recommended in the case of a long standing crown-root fracture involving the floor of the pulp chamber. The lower second molar is the most frequent tooth to fracture in vivo (Cavel *et al.,* 1985). A localised pocket in an otherwise periodontally uninvolved dentition is suggestive of a cracked or fractured tooth.

The mesio-occlusal portion of the amalgam restoration was removed and the floor of the pulp chamber examined. A fracture line was seen running from the mesial to the distal aspect of the tooth. Bleeding into the fracture line was evident (**162B**). The tooth was deemed to be beyond restoration.

163 Spreaders should be capable of reaching to within 1–2mm of the prepared apical stop alongside the master gutta percha cone to improve the quality of the seal (Allison et al, 1979).

A variety of spreaders of different lengths and widths are therefore required.

164 The symptoms can usually be relieved by placing a paste medicament, such as corticosteroid-antibiotic paste, into the canal. Then, further paste medicaments, such as a 50:50 mixture of corticosteroid-antibiotic paste and calcium hydroxide, or just calcium hydroxide alone, can be used for 3–6 months. This allows time for diffusion of the paste components and for radiographic follow up. In this particular case, the other canal in the same root (i.e. the mesio-buccal canal) could be fully negotiated so the situation was more favourable for repair. Reduction in size of the radiolucency indicates that the bacteria have been eliminated and the canal can then be filled to the level of the fractured file, as in this case (**164B**). However, if the radiolucency does not reduce in size, a more radical approach may be indicated, such as periapical surgery, root resection or extraction.

165 Generally, a pulpectomy is less successful than a pulpotomy in a primary tooth. This is probably due to the poorer condition of the pulp tissue at the time of the pulp therapy.

Although extremely high success rates have been reported in the literature, the findings must be viewed with caution because the extent and nature of the pathological changes were not always given, or even known by the investigator and also the conditions varied in the different studies. Further, the criteria used to determine success were not the same in each study; they may or may not have included freedom from pain, mobility, radiographic evidence of bone regeneration and internal resorption.

166 (a) If the child has a medical disorder which may lead to complications if the pulp therapy fails, or is partially successful, for example, patients who have cardiac defects, or have undergone transplant surgery.
(b) If there is caries in the root canals, because this is likely to lead to bacterial invasion of the root canals and the carious dentine cannot be removed adequately or without possibly perforating the root.
(c) If the crown of the tooth cannot be adequately restored after the pulp therapy. Provided 2–3mm of sound tooth substance remains in the cervical region of the crown a stainless steel crown can be fitted.
(d) When there is internal resorption in a root canal because this is generally irreversible.
(e) When a half to two-thirds of the roots are remaining it is often best to extract the tooth rather than to carry out pulp therapy.

167 The denseness of the maxillary bone, especially the zygomatic process does not allow adequate penetration of X-rays.

The use of an electronic root canal measuring device would be useful in this situation.

168 One explanation for this problem is that the tolerance to which the files are made is variable. This lack of standardisation may at least partly account for this observation.

A second explanation is that the increase in size from one file to the next is too large and that intermediary sizes may be desirable.

On occasions the apparent inability to place a file to the full length may be due to a mismatch of the curvature placed on the file and that of the canal. The inherent flexibility of the smaller files allows them to negotiate the canals despite having mismatched curves. This problem can be overcome by adjusting the degree of curvature of the files.

Intermediary sized files can be created by cutting approximately 1mm off the tip of the file and rounding off the sharp edges. A range of file sizes with identical taper can thus be created. Another solution is to use two different types of files which are manufactured to different diameters or tapers for given ISO sizes. For example, Hedstroem files are usually slightly narrower than K-Flex files. These instruments can then be used alternately to advance the canal in size without resorting to either over filing with the smaller files or using excessive force with the larger files.

169 Rubber dam should be used at all times in endodontic therapy to protect the patient from possible inhalation or ingestion of instruments, medicaments, tooth and filling debris and necrotic and infected material.

Rubber dam also provides a clean, dry, field of operation free from salivary contamination and unobstructed by tongue and cheeks.

Rubber dam dispenses with the need for talking and washing out and generally improves the efficiency of the operation.

170 The endodontic handpiece is called the Excalibur (W&H).

The handpiece produces a random lateral vibratory movement. The instruments used are modified K-type files and the handpiece is run at 20,000–25,000 rpm.

171 Extrusion of any material into the inferior dental canal may cause severe pain and alteration of sensation, ranging from paraesthesia to anaesthesia. The duration of these changes is dependent on the physical trauma of the incident, including the pressure under which the material was extruded and the chemical nature of the material. Certain resorbable, non-toxic materials are likely to show spontaneous recovery provided the physical trauma was minimal. The presence of toxic materials such as those containing paraformaldehyde may require surgery to remove the material as soon as possible to prevent irreversible damage to the inferior dental nerve. The morbidity of the surgical procedure must also be taken into consideration.

172 It may be necessary to soften the gutta percha with chloroform, xylol, or rectified turpentine. These solvents act on a small portion of gutta percha at a time and the process of removal may be very tedious.

The bulk of the gutta percha may also be removed by the use of a heated spreader or Gates–Glidden drills or a combination of the two methods. These methods are rapid and relatively safe.

173 (a) The separated instrument looks like a spiral filler. Its location suggests that the canal was perforated resulting in the instrument being lodged in alveolar bone.
(b) Since the post crown and root filling was satisfactory, it was decided to employ a surgical approach to remove the lodged instrument and repair the perforation. The separated instrument turned out to be a 5mm length of spiral filler and the perforation was repaired with amalgam.

174 Recurrent Herpes simplex. The appearance and the location of the lesion bears no apparent relation to the root filling in the lateral incisor. A detailed history and clinical examination revealed that the lesion first appeared as vesicles. Typically, recurrent Herpes simplex affects periosteal-bound, keratinized mucosa, *viz.* attached gingivae and the hard palate (**174A, 174C**).
The tenderness to palpation of the lateral incisor was attributable to the slight overfilling, which gradually subsided.

175 Paste-type medicaments work in several ways:
(a) By direct contact with the bacteria or tissues in the root canal.
(b) By diffusion through the dentinal tubules and accessory canals (and thereby contacting peripheral bacteria).
(c) By diffusion through the apical foramen to contact the periapical tissues.
(d) By some contact with the lateral periodontal ligament which also occurs via diffusion through the dentine and cementum.

176 This is a proliferative lesion of the dental pulp referred to as hyperplastic pulpitis or a pulp polyp. The proliferation is due to chronic irritation of a vascular pulp with a large exposure.

This condition is usually treated by root canal treatment, unless coronal damage does not permit restoration, in which case extraction is indicated. Pulpotomy has been advocated as a treatment regime in selected cases (Caliskan, 1993).

177 The upper left central incisor has a wide open apex. Conventional preparation and filling would lead to gross over-filling.

Apical closure can be induced by repeated dressing changes of calcium hydroxide over a 6–18 month period.

Ultimately the canal can be filled conventionally following the radiographic confirmation of apical closure.

178 The smear layer is formed as a result of the deformation of the surface of the dentine by the action of a metallic instrument. It consists of both inorganic and organic material derived from the pulp, dentine and any other material introduced into the canal, and can be divided into two layers. The superficial layer is loosely adherent and the deep layer is not only adherent to the dentine surface but is actually a 'smear' of it.

The clinical importance of this layer is a matter of conjecture. One school of thought holds that it harbours bacteria and prevents good adaptation of the root filling material to the wall and therefore should be removed. The other suggests that good clinical results are achievable without its removal and that its removal may simply allow penetration of bacteria into the dentinal tubules in the event of a subsequent recontamination. This could render re-treatment less successful and so the smear layer should not be removed. There is no conclusive proof for either argument.

179 (a) Treatment options include:
    (i) Extraction and prosthetic replacement.
    (ii) Re-root end resection and root end filling.
    (iii) Dismantling the bridge and carrying out conventional root canal treatment.
(b) Option (iii). Where possible, conventional root canal treatment is the treatment of choice. However, root end resection and root end filling has already been performed.

Conventional root canal treatment was carried out by dismantling the bridge and the sinus disappeared.

180 If the blood supply to the pulp is suddenly severed due to a traumatic injury and the root canal space is not subsequently infected, there may be no radiographically visible periapical change. Occasionally, there may be slight thickening of the periodontal ligament space (Bergenholtz, 1974).

181 The upper first molar has been heavily restored in the past. The commencement of root treatment has led to further weakening of the tooth, which has become susceptible to fracture. The longitudinal fracture involves the floor of the pulp chamber (**181B**). Treatment options are extraction and tooth resection.

182 (a) The advantages of marsupialisation (decompression) of large lesions are:

(i) Does not jeopardise pulpal vitality of adjacent teeth.

(ii) Does not damage adjacent anatomical structures when treating large lesions.

(b) The disadvantages include:

(i) Slower to heal than enucleation.

(ii) Demands patient's compliance with post surgical care.

183 Both radiopacities are retrograde root fillings. Two different materials have been used. A retrograde amalgam was placed in the upper right central incisor while the lateral incisor was filled with retrograde IRM.

Intermediate restorative material (IRM) and super-EBA cement are advocated as alternative materials for retrograde filling. The use of these materials as root end sealing agents has been shown to produce favourable results (Dorn and Gartner, 1990).

184 (a) Surgical endodontics was poorly executed. There is radiographic evidence of root filling material in the apical area. The root end filling and cavity was inadequate. Premolar teeth have oval shaped canals and cavity preparation should be extended accordingly.

(b) (i) Removal of post crown and carry out re-treatment.

(ii) Extraction and prosthetic replacement.

(iii) Repeat root end resection and root end filling.

(c) Option (iii). Since the post crown and root filling was adequate, yet failure has occurred, surgical endodontics should be repeated. If properly carried out to correct the previous shortcomings, the outcome is likely to be successful.

185 Radiography.
  Palpation.
  Percussion.
  Mobility.
  Biting.
  Fibre-optic light.
  Pulp testing:
      electric pulp tester
      heat
      cold.
  Local anaesthetic.
  Caries removal.
  Cutting a test cavity.
  Further tests e.g.:
      check cementation failure of crowns and bridges
      remove restoration and place a sedative dressing
      remove restoration to examine for caries or fracture
      fit diagnostic occlusal splint.

186 The tooth has been restored with posts in the mesial and distal roots. The posts do not appear to be within the canal space. Perforation of both posts into the periodontal tissues of the furcation is suspected as the likely cause of the patient's problems.

  The prognosis is poor.

187 The opacities are flaws created by faulty processing. The film was processed manually and drops of fixer solution had splashed on to the film before it was placed in the developer.

188 Medicaments may be utilised in endodontic therapy to:
(a) Help eliminate bacteria.
(b) Reduce inflammation (and thereby reduce pain).
(c) Induce healing of calcified tissues.
(d) Help eliminate apical exudate.
(e) Control inflammatory root resorption.
(f) Control contamination of canals between visits.

189 The swellings are bony protuberances or exostoses. They are usually found on the buccal aspect of the maxillary and/or mandibular alveolar ridges, presenting as multiple hard nodules. The surface mucosa is firm, taut, and without sign of inflammation. The vitality of teeth is not affected by this condition.

190 (a) The tooth is root filled and restored with a post crown. There is a radiolucent periradicular area.

(b) Whenever possible, removal of the post crown and re-treatment is preferable. However, in this case, an attempt to remove a post of this size and length is likely to damage or fracture the root. A surgical approach was therefore indicated.

191 (a) The Peeso reamer is the instrument of choice. It has a non-cutting tip which reduces the risk of perforation.

192 (a) Old perforations with bone loss in the furcation are difficult to treat and the prognosis is very poor (Gutmann *et al.*, 1988). By the time a radiolucency is evident in the furcation the defect is usually probeable (as illustrated). Surgical repair is inadvisable and root resection, hemisection or extraction should be considered. Non-surgical treatment would involve cleaning the pulp chamber to place calcium hydroxide over the perforation site, sealing the access cavity for a few days to provide a dry field. The perforation can then be sealed using a suitable restorative material, such as a glass ionomer, and the rest of the root filling completed.

(b) Provided the perforation is dealt with promptly and the contamination is minimal the prognosis is good. The perforation orifice is cleaned and dried without disturbing the furcation tissues and then sealed with a suitable restoration such as glass ionomer.

193 The condition is periapical cemental dysplasia. There is a large periapical radiolucency the central portion of which is radiopaque due to the deposition of cementum.

In the early stages the lesion resembles that of a periapical lesion of endodontic origin. This may account for the root treatment performed to the lower left central incisor.

194 The final shape of the root canal is dictated by its original shape which is modified to allow access to all aspects of its internal form for cleaning and irrigation. The amount of dentine which needs to be removed to achieve satisfactory debridement has not been properly established, but it is generally accepted that it is only necessary to remove a minimal amount compatible with removal of the bulk of bacterial presence and possibly their toxins.

In addition, the final shape of the root canal should also be compatible with the method of obturation to be employed, taking into consideration the properties of the material and access for the instruments which are necessary. For example, satisfactory obturation with lateral condensation of gutta percha demands that the spreaders can be placed to the desired lengths without binding against the canal walls. To take another example, satisfactory obturation using the Ultrafil thermoplasticised gutta percha technique requires that the canal is modified to facilitate the placement of the Ultrafil syringe cannule to within 4–5mm of the working length.

195 (a) The upper left central incisor is fractured and there is an endodontic (diodontic) implant in the tooth. Between the central incisors there is a large circumscribed radiolucent area. The position and radiographic appearance of the lesion suggests a nasopalatine cyst. The upper right central incisor should be vitality tested.

(b) Excision biopsy to enucleate the lesion and histopathology to confirm whether it is a nasopalatine cyst. No active treatment is required for the upper left central incisor since the symptoms are not related to this tooth. The tooth should be monitored (Abrams *et al.*, 1963; Allard *et al.*, 1981; Larsen *et al.*, 1989; Feldman and Feldman, 1992).

196 (a) The role of surgery in endodontics is well documented. However, it is now recognised that there are only a few true indications for surgical endodontics. These indications are:

(i) To establish drainage.

(ii) Following failure of conventional root canal treatment or re-treatment.

(iii) Need for biopsy or exploratory investigation, e.g. sinister pathology.

(iv) When conventional root canal treatment or re-treatment is impracticable.

(v) Expediency. This is not an absolute indication.

(b) Apart from general contra-indications, local contra-indications need to be considered. The following are local contra-indications to surgical endodontics:

(i) Poor access or visibility of the surgical site.

(ii) Anatomical and neurovascular considerations which might complicate surgery.

(iii) Presence of acute inflammation. Except to carry out incision and drainage, elective surgical endodontics should not be performed when there is acute inflammation.

(c) A pre-operative assessment before deciding to perform endodontic surgery should take into account the following factors:

(i) Medical history of the patient and associated drug therapy.

(ii) The possibility of conventional root canal treatment or re-treatment.

(iii) The position of the tooth and related anatomy including the proximity of neurovascular bundles.

(iv) Access and visibility of the surgical field

197 If an impacted tooth is fully embedded, signs of inflammation would not be discernible.

Occlusal, vertical and horizontal parallax radiography is most useful in the diagnosis of impacted teeth and odontomes. This impacted tooth was palpable and it was not necessary to use a parallax technique to locate it.

198 Those of endodontic origin. Periodontal defects of pulpal origin are associated with a necrotic pulp. The prognosis depends upon the success of the root canal treatment. Probing defects and mobility disappear very quickly.

199 Taking a careful history of the patients complaint can save a lot of time in the diagnosis and treatment. This patient has given the classical symptoms of a vertical fracture of the crown of the tooth before the pulp has become involved.

The patient should be asked if he feels pain when he bites down onto food or when he is releasing the bite. Many patients will report that they only feel pain when they are opening their mouth after completing the chewing cycle. The explanation may be that the fracture line closes as the pressure is released and fluid is compressed into the dentinal tubules, so affecting the pulp.

There are two methods of locating these early fractures, asking the patient to bite on a wood stick or rubber wheel and transilluminating the tooth with a fibre-optic light.

The stick or rubber wheel is used, first placing it in between the teeth on selected cusps, and asking the patient to bite and then release. If there is any pain the fibre-optic light is used. Many teeth may show enamel crazing but the more serious fracture involving dentine will in time become stained. The light from the fibre optic source will pass through the tooth but be partially blocked by the stain. This makes the fracture line clearly visible. If such a crack is located then any restoration in the tooth is removed and the floor of the cavity is examined. Sometimes the fracture can be seen on the floor of the cavity undermining a particular cusp. The cusp should be reduced and a temporary restoration piaced. If the symptoms disappear the tooth may have a cusp-covered inlay fitted which should prevent further propagation of the crack. An early vertical fracture, usually running sagitally, is treated by reducing all the cusps and either placing a temporary dressing or providing a temporary crown. The most common tooth to fracture is the mandibular second molar.

200 This could be considered an unfair question, because the state of the pulp can only be diagnosed with certainty by extirpation and examination under a microscope. There is no correlation between clinical findings and histology of the pulp (Dummer,1980). Surprisingly, there is also no correlation between the severity of pain and the extent of pulpal involvement (Mumford, 1967).

Clinical evaluation of the state of the pulp must rely entirely on the experience and acumen of the operator and, at best, mistakes will be made from time to time.

201 The acoustic streaming effect, which allows a fast and efficient replacement of the irrigant.

References

ABBOTT, P V, HEITHERSAY, G S, HUME, W R (1988) Release and diffusion through human tooth roots in vitro of corticosteroid and tetracycline trace molecules from Ledermix paste. *Endodontics & Dental Traumatology,* 4: 55–62.

ABBOTT, P V, HUME, W R, HEITHERSAY, G S (1989) Effects of combining Ledermix and calcium hydroxide pastes on the diffusion of corticosteroid and tetracycline through human tooth roots in vitro. *Endodontics and Dental Traumatology,* 5:188–192.

ABBOTT, P V (1990) Medicaments: Aids to success in endodontics. Part 1. A review of the literature. *Australian Dental Journal,* 35:438–448.

ABBOTT, P V (1990) Medicaments: Aids to success in endodontics. Part 2. Clinical recommendations. *Australian Dental Journal,* 35:491–496.

ABOU-RASS, M, FRANK, A L, GLICK, D H (1980) The anticurvature filing method to prepare the curved root canal. *Journal of the American Dental Association,* 101:792–794.

ABRAMS, A M, HOWELL, F J, BULLOCK, W K (1963) Nasopalatine cysts. *Oral Surgery, Oral Medicine and Oral Pathology,* 16:306–332.

ALLARD, R H B, VAN DER KWAST, A M, VAN DER WAAL, I (1981) Nasopalatine duct cyst – review of the literature and report of 22 cases. *International Journal of Oral Surgery,* 10:447–461.

ALLISON, D A, WEBER, C R, WALTON, R E (1979) The influence of the method of canal preparation on the quality of apical and coronal obturation. *Journal of Endodontics,* 5:298–304.

ANDREASEN, J O, ANDREASEN, F M (1990) *Essentials of Traumatic Injuries to the Teeth.* Munksgaard, Copenhagen.

BENJAMIN, K A, DOWSON, J (1974) Incidence of two root canals in human mandibular incisor teeth. *Oral Surgery, Oral Medicine and Oral Pathology,* 38:122–126.

BERGENHOLTZ, G (1974) Micro-organisms from necrotic pulp of traumatized teeth. *Odontologisk Revy,* 25:347–358.

BERGENHOLTZ, G (1978) Effect of experimentally induced marginal periodontitis and periodontal scaling on the dental pulp. *Journal of Clinical Periodontology,* 5:59–73.

BURCH, J G, HULEN, S (1974) A study of the presence of accessory foramina and topography of molar furcations. *Oral Surgery, Oral medicine and Oral Pathology,* 38:451–455.

BYERS, M R, TAYLOR, P E, KHAYAT, B G, KIMBERLEY, C L (1990) Effects of injury and inflammation on pulpal and periapical nerves. *Journal of Endodontics,* 16:78–84.

CALISKAN, M K (1993) Success of pulpotomy in the management of hyperplastic pulpitis. *International Endodontic Journal,* 26:142–148.

CAVEL, W T, KELSEY, W P, BLANKENALL, R J (1985) An in vivo study of cuspal fracture. *Journal of Prosthetic Dentistry,* 53:38–41.

CHAMBERS, I G (1982) The role and methods of pulp testing in oral diagnosis: a review. *International Endodontic Journal,* 15:1–5.

CRUMP, M C, NATKIN, E (1970) Relationship of broken root canal instruments to endodontic case prognosis: a clinical investigation. *Journal of American Dental Association,* 80:1341–1347.

CVEK, M (1972) Treatment of non-vital permanent incisors with calcium hydroxide. 1. Follow-up of periapical repair and apical closure of immature roots. *Odontologisk Revy,* 23:27–44.

CVEK, M (1973) Treatment of non-vital permanent incisors with calcium hydroxide. II. Effect on external root resorption in luxated teeth compared with effect of root filling with gutta percha. A follow-up. *Odontologisk Revy,* 24:343–354.

CVEK, M (1974) Treatment of non-vital permanent incisors with calcium hydroxide. IV. Periodontal healing and closure of the root canal in the coronal fragment of teeth with intra-alveolar fracture and vital apical fragment. A follow-up. *Odontologisk Revy,* 25:239–246.

CVEK, M (1981) Endodontic treatment of traumatized teeth. IN: Andreasen JO, ed.,*Traumatic Injuries of the Teeth.* 2nd ed., Munksgaard, Copenhagen, pp. 321–384.

DORN, S, GARTNER, A (1990) Retrograde filling materials: a retrospective success-failure study of amalgam, EBA and IRM. *Journal of Endodontics,* 16:391–393.

DUMMER, P M H (1980) Clinical signs and symptoms in pulp disease. *International Endodontic Journal,* 13:27–35.

ENGSTROM, B, SPANGBERG, L (1967) Studies on root canal medicaments. I. Cytotoxic effects of root canal antiseptics. *Acta Odontologica Scandanavia,* 25:77–84.

EHRMANN, E H (1965) The effect of triamcinolone with tetracycline on the dental pulp and the apical periodontium. *Journal of Prosthetic Dentistry,* 15:144–152.

EHRMANN, E H, TYAS, M J (1990) Cracked tooth syndrome: diagnosis, treatment and correlation between symptoms and post extraction findings. *Australian Dental Journal,* 35:105–112.

FELDMAN, M, FELDMAN, G (1992) Endodontic stabilizers. *Journal of Endodontics,* 18:245–248.

FOX, J, MOODNIK, R M, GREENFIELD, E, ATKINSON, J S (1972) Filling root canals with files. Radiographic evaluation of 304 cases. *New York State Dental Journal,* 38:154–157.

GOERIG, A C, NEAVERTH, E J (1991) Case selection and treatment planning. In: Cohen S, Burns RC eds. *Pathways of the Pulp,* 5th edn., Mosby-Year Book, St. Louis, pp. 48–60.

GOLDMAN, M, DE VITRE, R, TENCA, J I (1984) A fresh look at posts and cores in multi- rooted teeth. *Compendium of Continuing Education in Dentistry,* 5:711–719.

GROSSMAN, L I (1968) Fate of endodontically treated teeth with fractured root canal instruments. *Journal of the British Endodontic Society,* 2:35–37.

GUTMANN, J L, DUMSHA, T C, LOVDAHL, P E (1988) *Problem Solving in Endodontics.* Year Book Medical Publishers Inc., Chicago.

HARRISON, J W, MADONIA, J V (1970) The antimicrobial effectiveness of parachlorophenol. *Oral Surgery, Oral Medicine and Oral Pathology,* 30:267–275.

HARRISON, J W, MADONIA, J V (1971) The toxicity of parachlorophenol. *Oral Surgery, Oral Medicine and Oral Pathology,* 32:90–99.

HEITHERSAY, G S (1975) Calcium hydroxide in the treatment of pulpless teeth with associated pathology. *Journal of the British Endodontic Society,* 8:74–93.

HEITHERSAY, G S (1985) Clinical endodontic and surgical management of tooth and associated bone resorption. *International Endodontic Journal,* 18:72–92.

HEITHERSAY, G S, HUME, W R, ABBOTT, P V (1990) Conventional root canal therapy, II: Intracanal medication. IN: Harty FJ, ed. *Endodontics in Clinical Practice*. 3rd edn., Wright Butterworth Scientific, pp. 162–185.

KLEVANT, F J H, EGGINK, C O (1983) The effect of canal preparation on periapical disease. *International Endodontic Journal*, 16: 68–75.

KRAMER, I R H (1960) The vascular architecture of the human dental pulp. *Archives of Oral Biology*, 2:177–189.

KRAMPER, B J, KAMINSKI, E J, OSETEK, E M, HEUER, M A (1984) A comparative study of the wound healing of three types of flap design used in periapical surgery. *Journal of Endodontics*, 10:17–25.

LANGELAND, K, RODRIGUES, H, DOWDEN, W (1974) Periodontal disease, bacteria and pulpal histopathology. *Oral Surgery, Oral Medicine and Oral Pathology*, 37:257–270.

LARSEN, R M, PATTEN, J R, WAYMAN, B E (1989) Endodontic endosseous implants: Case reports and update of materials. *Journal of Endodontics*, 15:496–500.

MUMFORD, J M (1967) Pain perception threshold on stimulating human teeth and the histological condition of the pulp. *British Dental Journal*, 123:427–433.

NAYYAR, A, WALTON, R E, LEONARD, L A (1980) An amalgam coronal-radicular dowel and core technique for endodontically treated posterior teeth. *Journal of Prosthetic Dentistry*, 43:511–515.

NEDDERMAN, T A, HARTWELL, G R, PORTELL, F R (1988) A comparison of root surfaces following apical root resection with various burs: scanning microscopic evaluation. *Journal of Endodontics*, 14:423–427.

PIERCE, A, LINDSKOG, S (1987) The effect of an antibiotic/corticosteroid paste on inflammatory root resorption in vivo. *Oral Surgery, Oral Medicine and Oral Pathology*, 64:216–220.

REES, R T, HARRIS, M (1978–79) Atypical odontalgia. *British Journal of Oral Surgery*, 16:212–218.

SAFAVI, K E, DOWDEN, D E, LANGELAND, K (1987) Influence of delayed coronal permanent restoration on endodontic prognosis. *Endodontics and Dental Traumatology*, 3:187–191.

SCHINDLER, W G, GULLICKSON, D C (1988) Rationale for the management of calcific metamorphosis secondary to traumatic injuries. *Journal of Endodontics*, 14:408–412.

SIMON, J H, GLICK, D H, FRANK, A L (1972) The relationship of endodontic-periodontic lesions. *Journal of Periodontology,* 43:202–208.

SKIDMORE, A E, BJORNDAL, A M (1971) Root canal morphology of the human mandibular first molar. *Oral Surgery, Oral Medicine and Oral Pathology,* 32:778–784.

STANDLEE, J P, CAPUTO, A A, HANSON, E C (1978) Retention of endodontic dowels: effects of cement, dowel length, diameter and design. *Journal of Prosthetic Dentistry,* 39:401–405.

TAGGER, M, SMUKLER, H (1977) Microscopic study of the pulps of human teeth following vital root resection. *Oral Surgery, Oral Medicine and Oral Pathology,* 44:96–105.

TAGGER, M, TAMSE, A, KATZ, A, KORZEN, B H (1984) Evaluation of the apical seal produced by a hybrid root canal filling method, combining lateral condensation and thermatic compaction. *Journal of Endodontics,* 10:299–303.

TROPE, M, ELFENBEIN, L, TRONSTAD, L (1986) Mandibular premolars with more than one root canal in different race groups. *Journal of Endodontics,* 12:343–345.

VERTUCCI, F J (1974) The endodontic significance of the mesiobuccal root of the maxillary first molar. *US Navy Medicine,* 63:29–31.

VERTUCCI, F J (1978) Root canal morphology of the mandibular premolars. *Journal of the American Dental Association,* 97:47–50.

WALKER, R T (1988) Root canal anatomy of mandibular first premolars in a southern Chinese population. *Endodontics and Dental Traumatology,* 4:226–228.

WALTON, R, TORABINEJAD, M (1989) *Principles and Practice of Endodontics.* A Saunders Core Textbook in Dentistry, pp. 422.

WEINE, F S, HEALEY, H J, THEISS, E P (1975) Endodontic emergency dilemma: leave tooth open or keep it closed? *Oral Surgery, Oral Medicine Oral Pathology,* 40:531–536.

YANG, Z P, YANG, S F, LIN, Y C, SHAY, J C, CHI, C Y (1988) C-shaped root canals in mandibular second molars in a Chinese study. *Endodontics and Dental Traumatology,* 4:160–163.

ZILLICH, R, DOWSON, J (1973) Root canal morphology of the mandibular first and second premolars. *Oral Surgery, Oral Medicine and Oral Pathology,* 36: 738–744.

Index

Numbers refer to question and answer numbers.

Abscess
–acute periapical 48, 121
–developmental grooves 20
–drainage 6
–pulpal involvement 29
Access cavity design 146
Acid-etch splinting 49
Acoustic streaming effect 201
Adrenaline 116
ALARA 35
Alloys 80
Alpha phase gutta percha 11
Amalgam
–coronal-radicular foundation 63
–exposed pulp 88
–leakage studies 22
–posts/cores 63
–retrograde 183
–root end fillings 22
–tattoo 122
Ameloblastoma 8
Anaesthesia see Local anaesthesia
Analytic Technology Pulp Tester 18
Ankylosis, subluxation 8, 15
Antibiotics 55
Antiseptic solutions, intracanal 52
Apex locators 30, 42
Apexification 46, 61, 147, 161, 177

Barbed broaches 152
Bevelling, root surface 150
Bleaching
–internal 161
–non-vital teeth 100, 106
Bone
–cysts, traumatic 56
–lodged instruments 173
–resorption see Resorption
–sclerosis 25
–surgical defects 109
Bony protuberances (exostoses) 189
Broaches, barbed 152
Buccal object rule 102
Burs 145

Calcification
–resorption 8
–root canal 1
Calcium hydroxide
–apexification 46, 61, 147, 161, 177
–debridement of pulpal debris 30
–hard tissue repair 69, 79
–large radiolucent lesions 137
–periodontal healing 129
–replantation 49, 83
Camphorated chlorophenol 52
Canal Master 81, 117, 124
Canals see Root canals
Cast restorations, loose 58
Cementoma, periapical 56

Cementum
–periapical dysplasia 193
–resorption 15
CGRP-IR nerve fibres 62
Cold lateral condensation 30
Condensers 67, 95
Corticosteroid-antibiotic compounds 10, 45, 69, 111, 137
Cracked tooth
–long term management 94
–syndrome 43
–wedge test 84
Crowns
–lower incisors 100
–post retained, fracture 4
Cysts
–calcifying odontogenic 73
–mucous retention (mucocoele) 158
–nasopalatine 195
–pressure resorption 8
–following pulpotomy 134
–radicular 127
–traumatic bone 56
–within granulomas 119

Decompression (marsupialization) 182
Demethylchlortetracycline (demeclocycline) 10
Dens invaginatus (dens in dente) 60
Dentinal tubules 7
Dentinal wall smear layer 178
Dentine
–resorption 15
–secondary deposits 108
Dentinogenesis imperfecta 41
Discolouration 100, 106
–causes 149
–gingivae 122
–internal bleaching 161

Electric pulp test 68
Electronic apex locators 30, 42
Endocarditis, infective 55
Endotec thermal endodontic condenser 67
Enucleation, surgical 73
Excalibur handpiece 170
Exostoses 189
Extrusive displacement 5, 132
Exudate, haemorrhagic/purulent 96

Facial pain, atypical 97
Felypressin 116
Fibroma, ossifying 56
Files
–Hedstroem 124, 138, 168
–K-Flex 138, 168
–sizes 168
Fistulas, facial 36
Flaps
–design 51, 64, 71, 128
–mucoperiosteal rectangular 71
Flex-R 124

Flexogate 81
Force
–acute 8, 15
–chronic 15
Formaldehyde 89
Formocresol
–formulation 89
–pulpotomy 37, 77, 165
Fractures
–central incisor 195
–lower second molar 162
–root see Root fractures
–undiagnosed (cracked tooth syndrome) 43
–upper first molar 181
–vertical 13, 199
–visualizing 199

Gates Glidden 81
Giant cell lesions 119
Gingivae
–amalgam tattoo 122
–bleaching procedures 106
–herpes simplex infection 174
–swellings 189
Glycerine 89
Gold alloys 80
Granulomas
–cysts 119
–furcation 134
Grooves, congenital 7, 20
Gutta percha
–alpha phase 11
–condensers 95
–removal 172, 191
–syringes 85
–thermo-plasticised 30
Gutta percha points
–coated 59
–ingredients 107
–mismatched with file 16
–root canal sealer 44

Hand reamers 28
Handpieces 170
Healing
–failure 119
–radiographic evidence 87
Hedstroem files 124, 138, 168
Herpes simplex 174
Hodgkin's lymphoma 127
Hot vertical plugging 30
Hydrogen peroxide 106
Impacted teeth 197
–resorption 8
Implants, endodontic (diodontic) 195
Incision and drainage 96
Infection
–antibiotics 55
–formocresol 89
–herpes simplex 174
–post crown restorations 150
–post-root canal therapy 119
–primary molars 19
–resorption 8, 15
–root fracture 7

–roots 69
Inferior dental canal, extrusion of materials 171
Inflammation
–bone sclerosis 25
–periodontal ligament 14, 45, 131
–root resorption see Resorption
Injection systems 28
Instruments
–curved root canal preparation 117
–flexibility 160
–fractured 124, 150, 164
–root canal filling 95
–root canal preparation 81, 91, 117, 138
–separated 173
–smear layer 178
–ultrasonically energised 135
Inter-radicular lesions 104
Intermediate restorative material 183
Intra-oral palpation 130
Intracanal medication 10, 45, 46, 111, 147
–functions 175, 188
–irritation of periapical tissues 131
–volatile antiseptic solutions 52
Iodoform paste 165
–extrusion through apex 115

K-Flex file 138, 168
K-type reamer 138
Kilovoltage 32

Lamina dura 40
–loss of 65
Lateral canals 78
Lateral root perforation 90
Leubke-Ochsenbein (submarginal; rectangular) flap 51
Lignocaine hydrochloride 116
Local anaesthesia
–incision and drainage 96
–solutions 116
–vasoconstriction 139
Luxation, extrusive 5, 132

Marsupialization (decompression) 182
Maxillary lesions 73
Medication, intracanal see Intracanal medication
Mental foramen 120
Milliamperage 32
Monoamine-oxidase inhibitors 97
Mucocoele 158
Necrosis
–coagulative 77
–pulpal 5, 15, 180
Neoplastic lesions 127
Non-noble alloys 80
Non-vital teeth 41
–bleaching 100, 106

Occlusion trauma 15
Osteitis, condensing 65

Pain, diagnostic tests 185, 199
Palatal cleft, unilateral 156
Palladium rich alloys 80
Paper points 28
Parachlorophenol 52
Paraformaldehyde 52, 171
Paste materials, application 28

Peeso reamer 191
Perforation
–iatrogenic 7
–lateral root 90
–mesial canal 112
–periodontal tissues 186
–pulp chamber floor 108, 142, 192
–root canal 69, 173
–roots 17
–sub-alveolar 30
–supra-alveolar 30
Periapical bone resorption 8, 15, 62
Periapical cemental dysplasia 193
Periapical lesions 62, 140, 183, 193
–persistent 119
–treatment 137
Pericoronitis 103
Perio-endo lesions
–classification 34
–prognosis 136, 198
Periodontal ligament
–inflammation 14, 45, 131
–space 180
Periodontal pockets 104
Periodontitis, chronic apical 8, 15
Periodontium
–communication with pulp 7
–perforation 186
–pulp disease 14
Periradicular curettage 126
Periradicular lesions 182
Pink spot lesions 30, 53
Polyp, pulp 176
Post crown restoration 190
Posts
–amalgam 63
–fractured, removal 93
–minimum length 47
–perforation into periodontal tissues 186
–purpose of 21
–retention characteristics 50
–root fractures 125
–tooth weakening 100
Premolars, evaginated 39
Pressure resorption 8
Primary molars
–anatomical features 108
–chronic infection 19
Primary teeth
–carious, conservative treatment 9
–pulp therapy, contraindications 166
–pulpal involvement 29
Prophylaxis, antibiotic 55
Pulp
–clinical evaluation 200
–communication with periodontium 7
–debris, debridement 30
–dentinogenesis imperfecta 41
–disease and periodontal tissue 14
–extirpation 30, 131
–horn, locating 108
–necrosis 5, 15, 180
–polyp 176
–testers 18, 68

Pulp chamber
–cleaning 142
–drainage 105
–floor, perforation 108, 142, 192
–secondary dentine deposits 108
Pulpectomy 165
Pulpitis 86
–hyperplastic 176
–irreversible 31, 111
Pulpotomy
–failed 134
–formocresol 37, 77, 165
–restorations 155
–success rates 165

Radiography
–ALARA principles 35
–buccal object rule 102
–diagnosis 99
–faulty processing 187
–kilovoltage/milliamperage 32
–periapical 54
–recall 99
–treatment 99
–white line 40
–working length 102, 118, 167
Radiovisiography 70
Reamers 28
–K-type 138
–Peeso 191
Replantation 49, 83
–replacement resorption 8, 15, 49
–tooth storage 83
Resorption 8
–apical cementum 15
–apical dentine 15
–apical root 153
–calcification 8
–external 148
–external inflammatory 8, 61
–external replacement 8
–external surface 8
–idiopathic internal 30
–inflammatory 8, 23, 33, 45, 98
–internal 53, 148
–internal inflammatory 8, 129
–internal replacement 8
–orthodontic movement of teeth 133
–periapical 8, 15, 62
–pressure 8
–replacement 8, 15, 49
–root fractures 15
–trauma 15
Restorations
–post crown 190
–temporary 13
Retrograde fillings 183
Root canals
–anatomy 3
–apical enlargement 154
–apical foramina 7
–bacterial contamination 3, 45, 75
–bifurcated 2, 123, 143
–blockage 27
–C-shaped 38

–calcification 1
–curved 91, 112, 117
–instrumented, persistent exudate 66
–intracanal medication *see* Intracanal medication
–lateral 78
–ledges 16, 27
–locating 110, 144
–multiple 12, 57
–obturation (filling) 11, 13, 17
–perforation 69, 173
–preparation
—curved 91, 112, 117
—desired shape 194
—file size increases 168
—instruments 81, 91, 117, 138
—radiography 102, 118, 167
—step-back method 157
–sclerosis 144
–sealers 44
–second
—location 110
—lower second premolars 72
—mesio-buccal 12, 24
—missed in treatment 31, 92, 104
—upper premolars 92
–ultrasonic irrigation 135
–working length 16, 27, 102, 118, 167
Root end cavity preparation 101
Root end fillings 22
Root end resorption 15
Root fillings
–retreatment 26–
–retrograde 183
Root fractures 4, 66, 76, 159
–apical fragments 114
–caused by post placement 125
–infection 7
–resorption 15
–transverse 79
–traumatic 4, 76
Roots
–amputation, contraindications 151
–cysts 127
–infected 69
–lesions 104
–perforated 17, 90
–resection 88
–resorption *see* Resorption
–shortened 23, 33, 58
Rubber dams 169
–clamp placement 113

Sealer, ultrasonic application 135
Silver points 59, 61
Sinus tracts 17
–chronic draining 82

–discharging 190
–facial fistula 36
–intracanal medicaments 45
–pericoronitis 103
–persistent 58, 179
Smear layer 178
Sodium hypochlorite solution 30, 121
Spiral root fillers 28
Splinting
–extrusion 132
–replantation 49, 83
Split-dam technique 113
Spreaders 163
–ultrasonically activated 135
Super-EBA cement 183
Surgical endodontics 150, 184
–bone defects 109
–indications/contraindications 196
–post-surgical management 74
Sutures 141
Syringe, autoclavable 85

Teflon coated points 59
Temporary restorations 13
Thermomechanical compaction 95
Thermoplastic condensation technique 30
Titanium points 59
Trans-polyisoprene *see* Gutta percha
Transillumination 199
Trauma
–bone sclerosis 25
–chemical 8
–extrusive luxation 5, 132
–occlusion 15
–resorption lesions 8, 15
–root fractures *see* Root fractures
–tooth discolouration 149
–tooth replantation *see* Replantation
Traumatic bone cyst 56
Triamcinolone acetonide 10, 111
Tricresol 89
Tricyclic antidepressants 97

Ultrafil thermoplasticised gutta percha technique 194
Ultrasound
–acoustic streaming effect 201
–failed silver point 61
–fractured post removal 93
–instruments 135

Vasoconstriction 139

Wedge test 84

X-rays *see* Radiography

Zinc oxide
–dressings 77
–gutta percha points 107